Anonymous

Maundy Thursday and Good Friday services of the holy Apostolic Church of Armenia

Anonymous

Maundy Thursday and Good Friday services of the holy Apostolic Church of Armenia

ISBN/EAN: 9783337283407

Printed in Europe, USA, Canada, Australia, Japan

Cover: Foto ©Lupo / pixelio.de

More available books at **www.hansebooks.com**

Maundy Thursday

AND

Good Friday Services

OF THE

Holy Apostolic Church of Armenia.

Calcutta:
PRINTED BY THE CALCUTTA CENTRAL PRESS CO., LD.,
5, COUNCIL HOUSE STREET.
1888.

Notice.

THIS divine Service Book of the two great Solemn days, HOLY THURSDAY and GOOD FRIDAY is intended by the Armenian Priests of Calcutta for the use of *such* members of the Armenian Community who do not understand their language sufficiently well to follow the Services in the Church. The Priests trust that the book will meet with the approval of the said members of our Community, and that they will be benefited by it.

Index.

—o—

Renunciation—A Confession—A Form of Confession—Absolution—from page V to X.

HOLY THURSDAY—MORNING SERVICE.

	Page.
Lord's Prayer	1

PSALMS.

Lord how are they	2
O Lord God	2
Bless the Lord	3
Hear my prayer	5

ANTHEM.

I will wash	6

HYMN.

O Lord God	7

GOSPEL.

Now is my soul. St. John	8

HOLY THURSDAY—MIDDAY SERVICE.

PSALMS.

Unto Thee, O Lord	10
Judge me, O Lord	11
The Lord is	12
Unto thee will I cry	13
Give unto the Lord	14
I will extol thee	15
In thee, O Lord	16
Blessed is he	18
Fret not thyself	19

INDEX.

HOLY THURSDAY—MIDDAY—(Contd.)

	Page
O Lord	22
I said	23
I waited patiently	25
Blessed is he	26
As the hart panteth	26
Judge me, O God	27
As the hart panteth	36
O Give thanks	38
Make a joyful noise	39

LESSONS OF THE OLD TESTAMENT.

		Page
I cried by reason	(Jonah)	28
And the days	(Isaiah)	34
For I will take	(Ezekiel)	34

THE PRAYER OF MANASSES, KING OF JUDAH.

	Page
O Lord, Almighty God	29

HYMN OF St. MESROPE.

	Page
I beseech thee	32

ANTHEM.

	Page
Purge me with hyssop	32

GOSPEL.

		Page
Having therefore	(Hebrews)	35
And one of the	(St. Luke)	36

HOLY THURSDAY—SERVICE AT NOON.

	Page
Lord's Prayer	40

PSALMS.

	Page
Have mercy	40
Bow down	40

INDEX.

HOLY THURSDAY—NOON—(Contd.)   Page.
ANTHEM.

I will wash	40
His words	44
Thou preparest a table	49

LESSONS OF THE OLD TESTAMENT.

And it came	(Genesis)	40
The Spirit	(Isaiah)	42

GOSPEL.

And in those	(Acts)	43
After two days	(St. Mark)	46
For I have received	(Corinthians I.,)	49
Now the first day	(St. Mathew)	50

THE NICENE CREED.

We believe in one God	51

HOLY THURSDAY.—EVENING SERVICE.

Ceremony of Washing of Feet.

ANTHEM.

Purge me with hyssop. Have Mercy	53

PSALM.

The voice of the Lord. Give unto	55

LESSONS OF OLD TESTAMENT.

And the Lord spake	(Exodus)	55
Then made he ten lavers	(Kings I)	56
Fear not, O Jacob	(Isaiah)	57
Also he made	(Chronicles)	56

GOSPEL.

Moreover brethren	(Corinthians I)	58
Beloved, let us love	(John I)	58
Now before the feast	(St. John)	59
So after he had	(St. John)	64

INDEX.

HOLY THURSDAY—EVENING—(Contd.)
HYMN OF ST. NIERSES THE GRACEFUL.

	Page.
This day the Origin of Light Ineffable	61

HOLY THURSDAY—NIGHT SERVICE.

Our Father, &c.	64

PSALMS.

Lord how are they	64
O Lord God	65
Bless the Lord	66
Hear my prayer	67
Why do the heathen	70
Lord how are they	71
Hear me when I call	71
Blessed is he	85
As the hart panteth	86
Judge me O Lord	88
Deliver me from	94
O God thou hast	96
Hear my cry O God	97
O God the heathen are	103
Give ear, O Shepherd	104
Sing aloud unto God	105
Hold not thy peace, O God	110
The Lord said unto my Lord	112
Praise ye the Lord	113
O Give thanks	117
Have mercy upon me	127-32
Praise ye the Lord	128
Hold not thy peace	110

ANTHEM.

Praise ye the Lord	69
The rulers take counsel	72
An evil disease	88

INDEX.

HOLY THURSDAY—NIGHT—(Contd.)
                                                                             Page.

	Page
Deliver me from	97
They were rejected	106
They have spoken	114
O Give thanks	118
Princes have	122
Thou didst ride	124
I am up and go	129

HYMN OF ST. NIERSES THE GRACEFUL.

	Page
This day the Origin of Light Ineffable	72
He fulfilled the laws	88
With an affectionate	97
O Thou	106
O Thou the Releaser	114
His Hands were	118

GOSPEL.

		Page
Verily, Verily, I say unto you	(St. John)	74
Now the feast	(St. Luke)	90
And Jesus saith unto	(St. Mark)	99
Then saith Jesus	(St. Matthew)	108
And they that had	(St. Matthew)	115
And Judas also	(St. John)	120
Then led they Jesus	(St. John)	130

LESSON OF OLD TESTAMENT.

		Page
Blessed are thou O Lord	(Daniel)	124

SONG OF THE BLESSED VIRGIN MARY.

		Page
And my Spirit hath rejoiced	(St. Luke)	126

SONG OF THE ANGELS.

	Page
Glory to God in the highest	128

INDEX.

GOOD FRIDAY--MORNING SERVICE.

PSALMS.

	Page
Have mercy upon me, O God	133
Plead my cause, O Lord	133
O Lord, rebuke me not	136
Blessed is he	139
My God, my God	141
In thee, O Lord	145
Save me, O God	154
Hear my prayer, O Lord	162
Hear my prayer, O Lord	170

LESSONS OF OLD TESTAMENT.

		Page
And it was broken	(Zachariah)	135
The shew of their	(Isaiah)	138
The Lord God hath	(Isaiah)	140
And it shall come	(Amos)	144
Behold, my Servant	(Isaiah)	147
Who is this that	(Isaiah)	157
And the Lord hath	(Jeremiah)	164
And the Lord my God	(Zechariah)	171

GOSPEL.

		Page
But God forbid	(Galatians)	136
Let this mind be in you	(Phillippians)	138
For when we were	(Romans)	141
For the preaching	(Corinthians I)	144
For both he that	(Hebrews)	149
When the morning	(St. Matthew)	150
But Christ being	(Hebrews)	158
And straightway	(St. Mark)	159
Having therefore	(Hebrews)	166
And as soon as	(St. Luke)	166
I give the charge	(Timothy I)	172

INDEX.

GOOD FRIDAY.—EVENING SERVICE.

Our Father, &c. 174

PSALMS.

Bow down thine ear	... ...	175-198
Deliver me, O Lord	... ...	175-198
My God, my God	... ...	176-141
Let my prayer be	... ...	... 176
I will lift up	... (one verse) ...	... 176
For thou wilt	... (one verse) ...	... 177

ANTHEM.

They gave me also 175

LESSONS OF OLD TESTAMENT.

And the Lord	(Jeremiah) ...	... 175
Behold my Servants	(Isaiah) ...	... 175
For the ungodly said	(Solomon) ...	... 177
In that day	(Zachariah) ...	... 179

GOSPEL.

For it is better	(Peter I) ...	... 180
When the even was come	(St. Matthew) ...	... 180

TRISAGION.

Holy God, Holy and Mighty 181

PRAYER OF St. NIERSES THE GRACEFUL.

I confess with faith 182

THE SEVEN PENITENTIAL PSALMS 187

PSALMS.

Bow down thine ear	... ...	... 198
Deliver me O Lord	... ...	... 199

END.

Renunciation.

WE renounce Satan and all his devices, all his seductions, all his thoughts, all his ways, all his intentions, and his evil angels, all his wicked worship, all his seditious servants, and all his wicked power and influence, do we heartily renounce. (*Repeated thrice.*)

A CONFESSION

OF

The Orthodox Church of Armenia.

WE CONFESS and with our whole [most perfect] heart believe in the Father God, [Who is] not created, not begotten, but without beginning; [Who] also is begetter of the Son, and breather forth of the Holy Ghost. We believe in the Word God, [Who is] not created, [but] begotten and [Who has His] beginning from the Father, before the worlds. Who is neither posterior nor less; but as the Father is Father, so is the Son also Son. We believe in the Holy Ghost, [Who is] not created, [and] not of time; not begotten but breathed forth from the Father, of the same essence with the Father, and of the same glory with the Son. We believe in the Holy Trinity, One Nature, one Godhead—not three Gods, but One God— one will, one kingdom, one sovereignty, Maker of things, visible and invisible. We believe in a Holy Church, a remission of sins, a communion of saints. We believe [that] One of the three Persons, the Word God, begotten of the Father before the worlds, in time came down into the Mother of God [Deipora], the Virgin Mary, took of her blood and united it with His Godhead [Divinity], patiently tarried nine months in the Womb of that pure Virgin, and was made [or became] perfect man in spirit [or soul], and mind and body; one person, one figure [or appearance], and united in one nature. God was made [or became] man, without change, without alteration; conception without seed, and generation without corruption. So that as there is no beginning to His Godhead [Divinity], so also is there no end to His humanity; for Jesus Christ, yesterday and to-day, is the same and for ever. We believe [that] our Lord Jesus Christ, having gone about in the Earth, after thirty years came to Baptism; [that] the Father bare witness: "This is My Beloved Son," and the Holy Ghost like a dove came down upon Him. [That] He was tempted of Satan, and overcame him; preached the salvation of men, laboured in the body, hungered and thirsted; after that, of His own free will came into sufferings, was crucified, dead in the body, but alive in his Godhead [Divinity]. His body was laid in the grave united with His Godhead [Divinity]; and in spirit He went down into hell in His undivided Godhead [Divinity], preached to the spirits, spoiled hell, and set free the spirits. After three days He rose again from the dead, and appeared to the disciples. We believe [that] our Lord Jesus Christ went up into heaven in that same body, and sat at the right hand of God; and that he is to come in the same body, and in the glory of the Father, to judge the quick and dead; that is also the Resurrection of all men. We believe also in the retribution for works [done in the body]; to the righteous, life everlasting; and to sinners, everlasting torments.

A Form of Confession.*

I HAVE sinned against the most Holy Trinity, the Father, the Son and the Holy Ghost. I have sinned against God. I confess before God, and the Holy Mother of God, and in your presence, Revd. Father, all the sins that I have committed. Because I have

---

* In this form of Confession are represented all kinds of sins that human nature might commit under temptation; but in private confession the penitent must confess to the priest those sins *only* which he (or she) has committed.

sinned by thought, word and deed, willingly and unwillingly, knowingly and unknowingly; by all these I have sinned against God.

I have sinned by my soul and its influence, by my mind and its emotion, by my body and its sensation. I have sinned by the influence of my soul. I have sinned by cunning, by malignity, by insolence and timidity, by extravagance and niggardliness, by excessive addiction to appetite, by injustice, by proneness to evil, by despondency and mistrust; by all these I have sinned against God.

I have sinned by the evil employment of my tongue, by speaking lies, by taking false oaths, by swearing, by contention, by wrangling, by slander, by detraction, by spreading evil and malicious reports, by false accusation, by mockery, by raillery, by derision, by sowing discord and division, by imprecation, by cursing, by malediction, by murmuring, by being discontented, by speaking ill of others, by calumniating, by defaming, by backbiting, by censuring malignantly, by blaspheming; by all these I have sinned against God.

I have sinned by the evil employment of my hands, by stealing, by coveting, by robbing, by beating, by killing, by dragging; by all these I have sinned against God.

I have sinned with all the joints of my frame and with all the members of my body, with my seven senses and with my six sensations, and by all sorts of carnal inclinations and sensual desires, despising the virtuous conduct of my predecessors and becoming a bad example to those that are to come hereafter; by all these I have sinned against God.

I have, moreover, sinned by seven mortal sins; namely, by pride and all its parts, by malice and all its parts, by anger and all its parts, by idleness and all its parts, by avarice and all its parts, by gluttony and all its parts, by fornication and all its parts; by all these I have sinned against God.

I have, moreover, sinned against all the commandments of God, both by commission and by omission; for neither did I fulfil what I had undertaken to perform, nor did I avoid what I had promised to renounce! I embraced the laws, but neglected to abide by the laws. I was admitted into the order of Christianity, but was found unworthy by my deeds. I have knowingly and willingly followed the evil, and blindly neglected the good. Woe to me! woe to me!! woe to me!!! How can I enumerate the multitude of my sins? How can I confess the magnitude of my transgressions? For innumerable are my sins, inexpressible are my iniquities, unpardonable are my crimes, and incurable are my wounds! Oh! I have grievously offended my God and my Saviour!

Reverend Father, I hold thee as a medium of reconciliation and as an intercessor to the only begotten

Son of God, beseeching you that by the authority committed to you, you should absolve me from all my sins.

Absolution.

MAY the Merciful God have mercy upon you and forgive all the sins and offences which thou hast confessed and which thou hast omitted to confess, and I by virtue of the ministerial authority committed to me and of the divine commandment (*That whosesoever sins ye remit they are remitted unto them, and whosesoever sins ye retain they are retained) by the tenor of this text. I absolve thee from all thy sins committed by thought, word, and deed in the name of the Father, and of the Son, and of the Holy Ghost. I do moreover design thee to the sacraments of the Holy Church, that all thy good deeds may be considered as acts of benevolence conducive to the eternal life and spiritual beatitude. Amen.

---

* St. Job xx. vrs. 23. St. Matthew xvi. vrs. 19, and xviii. vrs. 18. 1 Cor. v. vrs. 1—6.

Maundy Thursday and Good Friday Services

OF THE

Holy Apostolic Church of Armenia

HOLY THURSDAY MORNING.

BLESSED is our Lord Jesus Christ. Amen.

OUR FATHER, who art in heaven, hallowed be thy name; thy kingdom come, thy will be done on earth, as it is in heaven. Give us this day our daily bread; and forgive us our trespasses, as we forgive them who trespass against us. And lead us not into temptation; but deliver us from evil. Amen.

Lord if thou wilt open my lips, my mouth shall sing forth thy Praise *(repeated twice.)* Blessed be the co-essential, simultaneous, indivisible Holy: Father, Son, and Holy Ghost. Now and ever world without end. Amen.

Psalm, iii, 1—8.

LORD, how are they increased that trouble me! Many are they that rise up against me. Many there be which say of my soul, There is no help for him in God. But thou, O Lord, art a shield for me; my glory, and the lifter up of mine head. I cried unto the Lord with my voice, and he heard me out of his holy hill. I laid me down and slept, I awaked; for the Lord sustained me. I will not be afraid of ten thousands of people that have set themselves against me round about. Arise, O Lord; save me, O my God: for thou hast smitten all mine enemies upon the cheekbone; thou hast broken the teeth of the ungodly. Salvation belongeth unto the Lord: thy blessing is upon thy people.

Psalm lxxxviii, 1—18.

O LORD God of my salvation, I have cried day and night before thee: Let my prayer come before thee: incline thine ear unto my cry: For my soul is full of troubles, and my life draweth nigh unto the grave. I am counted with them that go down into the pit; I am as a man that hath no strength: Free among the dead like the slain that lie in the grave, whom thou rememberest no more: and they are cut off from thy hand. Thou hast laid me in the lowest pit, in darkness, in the deeps. Thy wrath lieth hard upon me, and thou hast afflicted me with all thy waves. Thou hast put away mine acquaintance far from me; thou hast made me an abomination unto them. I am shut up, and I cannot come forth. Mine eye mourneth by reason of affliction: Lord, I have called daily upon thee, I have stretched out my hands unto thee. Wilt thou shew wonders to the dead? Shall the dead arise and praise thee? Shall thy loving kindness be declared in the grave; or thy faithfulness in destruction? Shall thy wonders be known in the dark; and thy righteousness in the land of forgetfulness? But unto thee have I cried, O Lord; and in the morning shall my prayer prevent thee. Lord, why castest thou off my soul? Why hidest thou thy face from me? I am afflicted and ready to die from my youth up; while I suffer thy terrors I am distracted. Thy fierce wrath goeth over me; thy terrors have cut me off. They come round about me daily like water; they compassed me about together. Lover and friend hast thou put far from me, and mine acquaintance into darkness.

Psalm ciii, 1—22.

BLESS the Lord, O my soul: and all that is within me, bless his holy name. Bless the Lord, O my soul, and forget not all his benefits: Who forgiveth all thine iniquities; who healeth all thy diseases; who redeemeth thy life from destruction; who crowneth thee with loving kindness and tender mercies; who satisfieth thy mouth with good things; so that thy youth is renewed like the eagle's. The Lord executeth righteousness and judgment for all that are oppressed. He made known his ways unto Moses, his acts unto the children of Israel. The Lord is merciful and gracious, slow to anger, and plenteous in mercy. He will not always chide: neither will he keep his anger for ever. He hath not dealt with us after our sins; nor rewarded us according to our iniquities. For as the heaven is high above the earth, so great is his mercy toward them that fear him. As far as the east is from the west, so far hath he removed our transgressions from us. Like as a father pitieth his children, so the Lord pitieth them that fear him. For he knoweth our frame; he remembereth that we are dust. As for man, his days are as grass: as a flower of the field, so he flourisheth. For the wind passeth over it, and it is gone; and the place thereof shall know it no more. But the mercy of the Lord is from everlasting to everlasting upon them that fear him, and his righteousness unto children's children; to such as keep his covenant, and to those that remember his commandments to do them. The Lord hath prepared his throne in the heavens; and his kingdom ruleth over all. Bless the Lord, ye his angels, that excel in strength, that do his commandments, hearkening unto the voice of his word. Bless ye the Lord, all ye his hosts; ye ministers of his, that do his pleasure. Bless the Lord, all his works in all places of his dominion: Bless the Lord, O my soul.

Psalm cxliii, 1—12.

HEAR my prayer, O Lord; give ear to my supplications: in thy faithfulness answer me, and in thy righteousness. And enter not into judgment with thy servant: for in thy sight shall no man living be justified. For the enemy hath persecuted my soul; he hath smitten my life down to the ground: he hath made me to dwell in darkness, as those that have been long dead. Therefore is my spirit overwhelmed within me; my heart within me is desolate. I remember the days of old; I meditate on all thy works; I muse on the work of thy hands. I stretch forth my hands unto thee: my soul thirsteth after thee, as a thirsty land. Hear me speedily, O Lord: my spirit faileth; hide not thy face from me, lest I be like unto them that go down into the pit. Cause me to hear thy loving kindness in the morning, for in thee do I trust: cause me to know the way wherein I should walk, for I lift up my soul unto thee. Deliver me, O Lord, from mine enemies: I flee unto thee to hide me. Teach me to do thy will; for thou art my God: thy spirit is good; lead me into the land of uprightness. Quicken me, O Lord, for thy name's sake: for thy righteousness' sake bring my soul out of trouble. And of thy mercy cut off mine enemies, and destroy all them that afflict my soul: for I am thy servant.

HOLY THURSDAY MORNING.

Glory be to the Father, and to the Son, and to the Holy Ghost. Now and ever world without end, Amen.

---o---

Hymns of St. Nierses the Graceful.
Litany.
Hymn of St. Nierses.
Prayer by the Priest.
Hymn of St. Isaac.
Litany.
Prayer by the Priest.

---o---

Anthem.

Alleluia, Alleluia, Alleluia.

Psalm, xxvi, 6—8.

I WILL wash mine hands in innocency: so will I compass thine altar, O Lord: Lord, I have loved the habitation of thy house, and the place where thine honour dwelleth.

Alleluia, Alleluia, Alleluia. Thou preparest a table before me in the presence of mine enemies: Thou anointest my head with oil; my cup runneth over.

Glory and blessing be to the Father, to the Son, and to the Holy Ghost. Now and ever, world without end. Amen. Alleluia (*repeated thrice.*)

A short Prayer by the Priest—"Our Father."

(*Prayers, Hymns and Psalms to follow here, see pages 124 p 8*):

Hymn.
Psalm, xciv, 1—23.

O LORD GOD, to whom vengeance belongeth; O God to whom vengeance belongeth, shew thyself. Lift up thyself, thou Judge of the earth: render a reward to the proud. Lord, how long shall the wicked, how long shall the wicked triumph? How long shall they utter and speak hard things, and all the workers of iniquity boast themselves? They break in pieces thy people, O Lord, and afflict thine heritage. They slay the widow and the stranger, and murder the fatherless. Yet they say, the Lord shall not see, neither shall the God of Jacob regard it. Understand, ye brutish among the people: and ye fools, when will ye be wise? He that planted the ear, shall he not hear? He that formed the eye, shall he not see? He that chastiseth the heathen, shall not he correct? He that teacheth man knowledge, shall not he know? The Lord knoweth the thoughts of man, that they are vanity. Blessed is the man whom thou chastenest, O Lord, and teachest him out of thy law; That thou mayest give him rest from the days of adversity, until the pit be digged for the wicked. For the Lord will not cast off his people, neither will he forsake his inheritance. But judgment shall return unto righteousness: and all the upright in heart shall follow it. Who will rise up for me against the evil-doers? Or who will stand up for me against the workers of iniquity? Unless the Lord had been my help, my soul had almost dwelt in silence. When I said, My foot slippeth; thy mercy, O Lord, help me up. In the multitude of my thoughts within me thy comforts delight my soul. Shall the throne of iniquity have fellowship with thee, which frameth mischief by a law? They gather themselves together against the soul of the righteous, and condemn the innocent blood. But the Lord is my defence; and my God is the rock of my refuge; and he shall bring upon them their iniquity, and shall cut them off in their own wickedness; yea, the Lord our God shall cut them off.

St. John, xii, 27—43.

NOW is my soul troubled; and what shall I say? Father, save me from this hour: but for this cause came I unto this hour. Father, glorify thy name. Then came there a voice from heaven, saying, I have both glorified it, and will glorify it again. The people therefore that stood by, and heard it, said that it thundered: others said, an angel spake to him. Jesus answered and said, This voice came not because of me, but for your sakes. Now is the judgment of this world: now shall the prince of this world be cast out. And I, if I be lifted up from the earth, will draw all men unto me. This he said, signifying what death he should die. The people answered him: We have heard out of the law that Christ abideth for ever: and how sayest thou, the Son of Man must be lifted up? Who is this Son of Man?

Then Jesus said unto them, Yet a little while is the light with you. Walk while ye have the light, lest darkness come upon you: for he that walketh in darkness knoweth not whither he goeth. While ye have light, believe in the light, that ye may be the children of light. These things spake Jesus, and departed, and did hide himself from them. But though he had done so many miracles before them, yet they believed not on him: That the saying of Esaias the prophet might be fulfilled, which he spake, Lord, who hath believed our report? and to whom hath the arm of the Lord been revealed? Therefore they could not believe, because that Esaias said again: He hath blinded their eyes, and hardened their heart; that they should not see with their eyes, nor understand with their heart, and be converted, and I should heal them. These things said Esaias, when he saw his glory, and spake of him. Nevertheless among the chief rulers also many believed on him; but because of the Pharisees they did not confess him, lest they should be put out of the synagogue: For they loved the praise of men more than the praise of God.

Exhortation by the Deacon, followed by a Prayer by the Priest.

HOLY THURSDAY MIDDAY.

Psalm li, " Have mercy upon me, &c."

Hymn of St. Nierses.
Prayer by the Priest.
Exhortation by the Deacon.
Prayer by the Priest.

Psalm, xxv, 1—22.

UNTO Thee, O Lord, do I lift up my soul. O my God, I trust in Thee: let me not be ashamed; let not mine enemies triumph over me. Yea, let none that wait on Thee be ashamed: let them be ashamed which transgress without cause. Shew me thy ways, O Lord; teach me thy paths. Lead me in thy truth, and teach me: for thou art the God of my salvation; on Thee do I wait all the day. Remember, O Lord, thy tender mercies and thy loving kindnesses; for they have been ever of old. Remember not the sins of my youth, nor my transgressions: according to thy mercy remember thou me for thy goodness' sake, O Lord. Good and upright is the Lord: therefore will He teach sinners in the way. The meek will He guide in judgment: and the meek will He teach his way. All the paths of the Lord are mercy and truth unto such as keep His covenant and His testimonies. For thy name's sake, O Lord, pardon mine iniquity; for it is great. What man is he that feareth the Lord? Him shall he teach in the way that he shall choose. His soul shall dwell at ease; and his seed shall inherit the earth. The secret of the Lord is with them that fear Him; and He will shew them his covenant. Mine eyes are ever toward the Lord; for he shall pluck my feet out of the net. Turn Thee unto me, and have mercy upon me; for I am desolate and afflicted. The troubles of my heart are enlarged: O bring thou me out of my distresses. Look upon my affliction and my pain; and forgive all my sins. Consider mine enemies; for they are many; and they hate me with cruel hatred. O keep my soul, and deliver me: let me not be ashamed; for I put my trust in Thee. Let integrity and uprightness preserve me; for I wait on Thee. Redeem Israel, O God, out of all his troubles.

Psalm, xxvi, 1—12.

JUDGE me, O Lord; for I have walked in mine integrity: I have trusted also in the Lord; therefore I shall not slide. Examine me, O Lord, and prove me; try my reins and my heart. For thy loving kindness is before mine eyes: and I have walked in thy truth. I have not sat with vain persons, neither will I go in with dissemblers. I have hated the congregation of evildoers; and will not sit with the wicked. I will wash mine hands in innocency: so will I compass thine altar O Lord: That I may publish with the voice of thanksgiving, and tell of all thy wondrous works. Lord, I have loved the habitation of thy house, and the place where thine honour dwelleth.

Gather not my soul with sinners, nor my life with bloody men. In whose hands is mischief, and their right hand is full of bribes. But as for me, I will walk in mine integrity; redeem me, and be merciful unto me. My foot standeth in an even place; in the congregations will I bless the Lord.

Psalm, xxvii, 1—14.

THE Lord is my light and my salvation, whom shall I fear? The Lord is the strength of my life, of whom shall I be afraid? When the wicked, even mine enemies and my foes, came upon me to eat up my flesh, they stumbled and fell. Though an host should encamp against me, my heart shall not fear: though war should rise against me, in this will I be the confident. One thing have I desired of the Lord, that will I seek after; that I may dwell in the house of the Lord all the days of my life, to behold the beauty of the Lord, and to enquire in his temple. For in the time of trouble he shall hide me in his pavilion: in the secret of his tabernacle shall he hide me; he shall set me up upon a rock. And now shall mine head be lifted up above mine enemies round about me: there-

HOLY THURSDAY MIDDAY.

fore will I offer in his tabernacle sacrifices of joy; I will sing, yea, I will sing praises unto the Lord. Hear, O Lord, when I cry with my voice: have mercy also upon me, and answer me. When thou saidst, seek ye my face; my heart said unto thee, Thy face, Lord, will I seek. Hide not thy face far from me; put not thy servant away in anger: thou hast been my help; leave me not, neither forsake me, O God of my salvation. When my father and my mother forsake me, then the Lord will take me up. Teach me thy way, O Lord, and lead me in a plain path, because of mine enemies. Deliver me not over unto the will of mine enemies: for false witnesses are risen up against me, and such as breathe out cruelty. I had fainted, unless I had believed to see the goodness of the Lord in the land of the living. Wait on the Lord: be of good courage, and he shall strengthen thine heart: wait, I say, on the Lord.

Glory be to the Father, and to the Son, and to the Holy Ghost. Now and ever world without end, Amen.

———o———

Prayer by the Deacon.
Prayer by the Priest.

———o———

Psalm, xxviii, 1—9.

UNTO thee will I cry, O Lord, my rock; be not silent to me: lest if thou be silent to me, I become like them that go down into the pit. Hear the voice of my supplications, when I cry unto thee, when I lift up my hands toward Thy holy oracle. Draw me not away with the wicked, and with the workers of iniquity, which speak peace to their neighbours, but mischief is in their hearts. Give them according to their deeds, and according to the wickedness of their endeavours: give them after the work of their hands, render to them their desert. Because they regard not the works of the Lord, nor the operation of his hands, he shall destroy them, and not build them up. Blessed be the Lord, because he hath heard the voice of my supplications. The Lord is my strength and my shield; my heart trusted in him, and I am helped: therefore my heart greatly rejoiceth; and with my song will I praise him. The Lord is their strength, and he is the saving strength of his Anointed. Save thy people, and bless thy inheritance: feed them also, and lift them up for ever.

Psalm, xxix, 1—11.

GIVE unto the Lord, O ye mighty, give unto the Lord glory and strength. Give unto the Lord the glory due unto his name; worship the Lord in the beauty of holiness. The voice of the Lord is upon the waters: the God of glory thundereth: the Lord is upon many waters. The voice of the Lord is powerful; the voice of the Lord is full of majesty. The voice of the Lord breaketh the cedars; yea the Lord breaketh the cedars of Lebanon. He maketh them also to skip like a calf; Lebanon and Sirion like a young unicorn. The voice of the Lord divideth the flames of fire. The voice of the Lord shaketh the wilderness; the Lord shaketh the wilderness of Kadesh. The voice of the Lord maketh the hinds to calve, and discovereth the forests: and in his temple doth every one speak of his glory. The Lord sitteth upon the flood; yea, the Lord sitteth King for ever. The Lord will give strength unto his people; the Lord will bless his people with peace.

Psalm, xxx, 1—12.

I WILL extol thee, O Lord, for thou hast lifted me up, and hast not made my foes to rejoice over me. O Lord my God, I cried unto thee, and thou hast healed me. O Lord, thou hast brought up my soul from the grave: thou hast kept me alive, that I should not go down to the pit. Sing unto the Lord, O ye saints of his, and give thanks at the remembrance of his holiness. For his anger endureth but a moment; in his favour is life: weeping may endure for a night, but joy cometh in the morning. And in my prosperity I said, I shall never be moved. Lord, by thy favour thou hast made my mountain to stand strong: thou didst hide thy face, and I was troubled. I cried to thee, O Lord, and unto the Lord I made supplication. What profit is there in my blood, when I go down to the pit? Shall the dust praise thee? Shall it declare thy truth? Hear, O Lord, and have mercy upon me: Lord be thou my helper. Thou hast turned for me my mourning into dancing: thou hast put off my sackcloth, and girded me with gladness. To the end that my glory may sing praise to thee, and not be silent. O Lord my God, I will give thanks unto thee for ever.

Glory be to the Father, and to the Son, and to the Holy Ghost. Now and ever, world without end, Amen.

Prayer by the Deacon.
Prayer by the Priest.

Psalm, xxxi, 1—24.

IN thee, O Lord, do I put my trust; let me never be ashamed: deliver me in thy righteousness. Bow down thine ear to me; deliver me speedily; be thou my strong rock, for an house of defence to save me. For thou art my rock and my fortress; therefore for thy name's sake lead me, and guide me. Pull me out of the net that they have laid privily for me: for thou art my strength. Into thine hand I commit my spirit, thou hast redeemed me, O Lord God of Truth. I have hated them that regard lying vanities: but I trust in the Lord. I will be glad and rejoice in thy mercy: for thou hast considered my trouble; thou hast known my soul in adversities; and hast not shut me up into the hand of the enemy: thou hast set my feet in a large room. Have mercy upon me, O Lord, consumed with grief, yea, my soul and my belly. For my life is spent with grief, and my years with sighing: my strength faileth because of mine iniquity, and my bones are consumed. I was a reproach among all mine enemies, but especially among my neighbours, and a fear to mine acquaintance: they that did see me without fled from me. I am forgotten as a dead man out of mind: I am like a broken vessel. For I have heard the slander of many; fear was on every side, while they took counsel together against me; they devised to take away my life. But I trusted in thee, O Lord: I said, Thou art my God. My times are in thy hand: deliver me from the hand of mine enemies, and from them that persecute me. Make thy face to shine upon thy servant; save me for thy mercies' sake. Let me not be ashamed, O Lord, for I have called upon thee: let the wicked be ashamed, and let them be silent in the grave. Let the lying lips be put to silence; which speak grievous things proudly and contemptuously against the righteous. Oh how great is thy goodness, which thou hast laid up for them that fear thee; which thou hast wrought for them that trust in thee before the sons of men. Thou shalt hide them in the secret of thy presence from the pride of man: thou shalt keep them secretly in a pavilion from the strife of tongues. Blessed be the Lord: for he hath shewn me his marvellous kindness in a strong city. For I said in my haste, I am cut off from before thine eyes: nevertheless thou heardest the voice of my supplications when I cried unto thee. O Love the Lord, all ye his saints; for the Lord preserveth the faithful, and plentifully rewardeth the proud-doer. Be of good courage, and he shall strengthen your heart, all ye that hope in the Lord.

Psalm, xxxii, 1—11.

BLESSED is he whose transgression is forgiven, whose sin is covered. Blessed is the man unto whom the Lord imputeth not iniquity, and in whose spirit there is no guile. When I kept silence, my bones waxed old through my roaring all the day long. For day and night thy hand was heavy upon me: my moisture is turned into the drought of summer. I acknowledged my sin unto thee, and mine iniquity have I not hid. I said, I will confess my transgressions unto the Lord, and thou forgavest the iniquity of my sin. For this shall every one that is godly pray unto thee in a time when thou mayest be found, surely in the floods of great waters they shall not come nigh unto him.

Thou art my hiding place; thou shalt preserve me from trouble; thou shalt compass me about with songs of deliverance. I will instruct thee and teach thee in the way which thou shalt go; I will guide thee with mine eye. Be ye not as the horse, or as the mule, which have no understanding: whose mouth must be held in with bit and bridle, lest they come near unto thee. Many sorrows shall be to the wicked; but he that trusteth in the Lord, mercy shall compass him about. Be glad in the Lord, and rejoice, ye righteous: and shout for joy, all ye that are upright in heart.

Glory be to the Father, and to the Son, and to the Holy Ghost. Now and ever, world without end, Amen.

---o---

Prayer by the Deacon.
Prayer by the Priest.

---o---

Psalm, xxxvii, 1—40.

FRET not thyself because of evil-doers, neither be thou envious against the workers of iniquity. For they shall soon be cut down like the grass, and wither as the green herb. Trust in the Lord, and do good; so shalt thou dwell in the land, and verily thou shalt be fed. Delight thyself also in the Lord; and he shall give thee the desires of thine heart. Commit thy way unto the Lord, trust also in him; and he shall bring it to pass. And he shall bring forth thy righteousness as the light, and thy judgment as the noonday. Rest in the Lord, and wait patiently for him; fret not thyself because of him who prospereth in his way, because of the man who bringeth wicked devices to pass. Cease from anger, and forsake wrath: fret not thyself in any wise to do evil. For evil-doers shall be cut off; but those that wait upon the Lord, they shall inherit the earth. For yet a little while, and the wicked shall not be: yea, thou shalt diligently consider his place, and it shall not be. But the meek shall inherit the earth; and shall delight themselves in the abundance of peace. The wicked plotteth against the just, and gnasheth upon him with his teeth. The Lord shall laugh at him; for he seeth that his day is coming. The wicked have drawn out the sword, and have bent their bow, to cast down the poor and needy, and to slay such as be of upright conversation. Their sword shall enter into their own heart, and their bows shall be broken. A little that a righteous man hath is better than the riches of many wicked. For the arms of the wicked shall be broken; but the Lord upholdeth the righteous. The Lord knoweth the days of the upright; and their inheritance shall be for ever. They shall not be ashamed in the evil time; and in the days of famine they shall be satisfied. But the wicked shall perish, and the enemies of the Lord shall be as the fat of lambs;. they shall consume ; into smoke shall they consume away. The wicked borroweth, and payeth not again ; but the righteous sheweth mercy, and giveth. For such as be blessed of him shall inherit the earth, and they that be cursed of him shall be cut off. The steps of a good man are ordered by the Lord, and he delighteth in his way. Though he fall, he shall not be utterly cast down : for the Lord upholdeth him with his hand. I have been young, and now am old ; yet have I not seen the righteous forsaken, nor his seed begging bread. He is ever merciful, and lendeth ; and his seed is blessed. Depart from evil, and do good ; and dwell for evermore. For the Lord loveth judgment, and forsaketh not his saints ; they are preserved for ever ; but the seed of the wicked shall be cut off. The righteous shall inherit the land, and dwell therein for ever. The mouth of the righteous speaketh wisdom, and his tongue talketh of judgment. The law of his God is in his heart ; none of his steps shall slide. The wicked watcheth the righteous, and seeketh to slay him. The Lord will not leave him in his hand, nor condemn him when he is judged. Wait on the Lord, and keep his way, and he shall exalt thee to inherit the land : when the wicked are cut off, thou shalt see it. I have seen the wicked in great power, and spreading himself like a green bay tree. Yet he passed away, and, lo ! he was not ; yea, I sought him, but he could not be found. Mark the perfect man, and behold the upright; for the end of that man is peace. But the transgressors shall be destroyed together: the end of the wicked shall be cut off. But the salvation of the righteous is of the Lord; he is their strength in the time of trouble. And the Lord shall help them, and deliver them; he shall deliver them from the wicked, and save them, because they trust in him.

Glory be to the Father and to the Son, and to the Holy Ghost. Now and ever, world without end, Amen.

—o—

Prayer by the Deacon.
Prayer by the Priest.

—o—

Psalm, xxxviii, 1—22.

O LORD, rebuke me not in thy wrath; neither chasten me in thy hot displeasure. For thine arrows stick fast in me, and thy hand presseth me sore. There is no soundness in my flesh because of thine anger; neither is there any rest in my bones because of my sin. For mine iniquities are gone over mine head; as a heavy burden they are too heavy for me. My wounds stink and are corrupt because of my foolishness. I am troubled; I am bowed down greatly; I go mourning all the day long. For my loins are filled with a loathsome disease; and there is no soundness in my flesh. I am feeble and sore broken: I have roared by reason of the disquietness of my heart. Lord, all my desire is before thee; and my groaning is not hid from thee. My heart panteth, my strength faileth me; as for the light of mine eyes, it also is gone from me. My lovers and my friends stand aloof from my sore; and my kinsmen stand afar off. They also that seek after my life lay snares for me; and they that seek my hurt speak mischievous things, and imagine deceits all the day long. But I, as a deaf man, heard not; and I was as a dumb man that openeth not his mouth. Thus I was as a man that heareth not, and in whose mouth are no reproofs. For in thee, O Lord, do I hope: thou wilt hear, O Lord my God. For I said, Hear me, lest otherwise they should rejoice over me; when my foot slippeth, they magnify themselves against me. For I am ready to halt, and my sorrow is continually before me. For I will declare mine iniquity; I will be sorry for my sin. But mine enemies are lively, and they are strong: and they that hate me wrongfully are multiplied. They also that render evil for good are mine adversaries; because I follow the thing that is good. Forsake me not, O Lord, O my God, be not far from me. Make haste to help me, O Lord my salvation.

Psalm, xxxix, 1—13.

I SAID, I will take heed to my ways, that I sin not with my tongue; I will keep my mouth with a bridle, while the wicked is before me. I was dumb with silence, I held my peace, even from good; and my sorrow was stirred. My heart was hot within me, while I was musing the fire burned; then spake I with my tongue, Lord, make me to know mine end, and the measure of my days, what it is; that I may know how frail I am. Behold, thou hast made my days as an hand breadth; and mine age is as nothing before thee: verily every man at his best state is altogether vanity. Surely every man walketh in a vain show; surely they are disquieted in vain: he heapeth up riches, and knoweth not who shall gather them. And now, Lord, what wait I for? My hope is in thee Deliver me from all my transgressions: make me not the reproach of the foolish. I was dumb, I opened not my mouth; because thou didst it. Remove thy stroke away from me; I am consumed by the blow of thine hand. When thou with rebukes dost correct man for iniquity, thou makest his beauty to consume away like a moth: surely every man is vanity. Hear my prayer, O Lord, and give ear unto my cry; hold not thy peace at my tears: for I am a stranger with thee, and a sojourner, as all my fathers were. O spare me, that I may recover strength, before I go hence, and be no more.

Psalm, xl, 1—17.

I WAITED patiently for the Lord; and he inclined unto me, and heard my cry. He brought me up also out of an horrible pit, out of the miry clay, and set

HOLY THURSDAY MIDDAY.

my feet upon a rock, and established my goings. And he hath put a new song in my mouth, even praise unto our God: many shall see it, and fear, and shall trust in the Lord. Blessed is the man that maketh the Lord his trust, and respecteth not the proud, nor such as turn aside to lies. Many, O Lord my God, are thy wonderful works which thou hast done, and thy thoughts which are to us—ward: they cannot be reckoned up in order unto thee: if I would declare and speak of them, they are more than can be numbered. Sacrifice and offering thou didst not desire; mine ears hast thou opened: burnt offering and sin offering hast thou not required. Then said I, Lo, I come: in the volume of the book it is written of me, I delight to do thy will, O my God: yea, thy law is within my heart. I have preached righteousness in the great congregation: lo, I have not refrained my lips, O Lord, thou knowest. I have not hid thy righteousness within my heart; I have declared thy faithfulness and thy salvation: I have not concealed thy loving kindness and thy truth from the great congregation. Withhold not thou thy tender mercies from me, O Lord: let thy loving kindness and thy truth continually preserve me. For innumerable evils have compassed me about: mine iniquities have taken hold upon me, so that I am not able to look up; they are more than the hairs of mine head: therefore my heart faileth me. Be pleased, O Lord, to deliver me: O Lord, make haste to help me. Let them be ashamed and confounded together that seek after my soul to destroy it: let them be driven backward and put to shame that wish me evil. Let them be desolate for a reward of their shame that say unto me, Aha, Aha. Let all those that seek thee rejoice and be glad in thee: let such as love thy salvation say continually, The Lord be magnified. But I am poor and needy; yet the Lord thinketh upon me: thou art my help and my deliverer; make no tarrying, O my God.

Glory be to the Father, and to the Son, and to the Holy Ghost, now and ever, world without end. Amen.

———o———

Prayer by the Deacon.
Prayer by the Priest.

———o———

Psalm, xli, 1—13.

BLESSED is he that considereth the poor; the Lord will deliver him in time of trouble. The Lord will preserve him, and keep him alive; and he shall be blessed upon the earth: and thou wilt not deliver him unto the will of his enemies. The Lord will strengthen him upon the bed of languishing. *(See page 71.)*

Psalm, xlii, 1—11.

AS the hart panteth after the water-brooks, so panteth my soul after thee, O God. My soul thirsteth for God, for the living God: when shall I come and appear before God? My tears have been my meat day and night, while they continually say unto me, Where is thy God? When I remember these things, I pour out my soul in me: for I had gone with the multitude. I went with them to the house of God, with the voice of joy and praise, with a multitude that kept holy day. Why art thou cast down, O my soul, and why art thou disquieted in me? Hope thou in God: for I shall yet praise him for the help of his countenance. O my God, my soul is cast down within me: therefore will I remember thee from the land of Jordan, and of the Hermonites from the hill Mizar. Deep calleth unto deep at the noise of thy waterspouts: all thy waves and thy billows are gone over me. Yet the Lord will command his loving kindness in the day time, and in the night his song shall be with me, and my prayer unto the God of my life. I will say unto God my rock, Why hast thou forgotten me? Why go I mourning because of the oppression of the enemy? As with a sword in my bones, mine enemies reproach me; while they say daily unto me, Where is thy God? Why art thou cast down, O my soul? and why art thou disquieted within me? hope thou in God: for I shall yet praise him, who is the health of my countenance, and my God.

Psalm, xliii, 1—5.

JUDGE me, O God, and plead my cause against an ungodly nation: O deliver me from the deceitful and unjust man. For thou art the God of my strength: why dost thou cast me off? Why go I mourning because of the oppression of the enemy? O send out thy light and thy truth: let them lead me; let them bring me unto thy holy hill, and to thy tabernacles. Then will I go unto the altar of God, unto God my exceeding joy: yea, upon the harp will I praise thee, O God my God. Why art thou cast down, O my soul? and why art thou disquieted within me? hope in God: for I shall yet praise him, who is the health of my countenance, and my God.

Glory be, to the Father, and to the Son, and to the Holy Ghost, now and ever, world without end. Amen.

———o———

Exhortation by the Deacon.
Prayer by the Priest.

———o———

Jonah, ii, 2—9.

I CRIED by reason of mine affliction unto the Lord, and he heard me; out of the belly of hell cried I, and thou heardest my voice. For thou hadst cast me into the deep, in the midst of the seas; and the floods compassed me about: all thy billows and thy waves passed over me. Then I said, I am cast out of thy sight; yet I will look again toward thy holy temple. The waters compassed me about, even to the soul: the depth closed me round about; the weeds were wrapped about my head. I went down to the bottoms of the mountains ; the earth with her bars was about me for ever : yet hast thou brought up my life from corruption, O Lord my God. When my soul fainted within me I remembered the Lord : and my prayer came in unto thee, into thine holy temple. They that observe lying vanities forsake their own mercy. But I will sacrifice unto thee with the voice of thanksgiving : I will pay that that I have vowed.

Glory be to the Father, and to the Son, and to the Holy Ghost, now and ever, world without end. Amen.

The priest and people kneeling down shall then sing the—

Hymn of St. Mesrope (repeated thrice).

—o—

Jonah, ii, 2—9. "I cried by reason, etc."

Hymn of St. Mesrope (repeated thrice.)

—o—

Jonah, ii, 2—9. "I cried by reason, etc."

Hymn of St. Mesrope (repeated thrice.)

—o—

The Prayer of Manasses,

King of Judah.

O LORD, Almighty God of our fathers, Abraham, Isaac, and Jacob, and of their righteous seed, Almighty Lord forgive me my sins. Who hast made heaven and earth, with all the ornament thereof, Almighty Lord forgive me my sins. Who hast bound the sea by the word of thy commandment; Almighty Lord forgive me my sins. Who hast shut up the deep, and sealed it by the terrible and glorious name; Almighty Lord forgive me my sins. Whom all men fear, and tremble before thy power; Almighty Lord forgive me my sins. For the majesty of thy glory cannot be borne, and thine angry threatening toward sinners is importable. But thy merciful promise is unmeasurable and unsearchable. Almighty Lord forgive me my sins. For thou art the most high Lord, of great compassion, long suffering, very merciful, and repentest of the evils of men. Almighty Lord forgive me my sins. Thou O Lord, according to thy great goodness hast promised repentance and forgiveness to them that have sinned against thee: and of thine infinite mercies hast appointed repentance unto sinners, that they may be saved. Almighty Lord forgive me my sins. Thou therefore, O Lord, that art the God of the just, hast not appointed repentance to the just, as to Abraham, and Isaac, and Jacob, which have not sinned against thee. Almighty Lord forgive me my sins. But thou hast appointed repentance unto me that am a sinner: for I have sinned above the number of the sands of the sea. Almighty Lord forgive me my sins. My transgressions, O Lord, are multiplied. Almighty Lord forgive me my sins. My transgressions are multiplied, and

I am not worthy to behold and see the height of heaven for the multitude of mine iniquities. Almighty Lord forgive me my sins. I am bound down with many iron bands, that I cannot lift up mine head, neither have any release: for I have provoked thy wrath, and pone evil before thee. Almighty Lord forgive me my sins. I did not thy will, neither kept I thy commandments. Almighty Lord forgive me my sins. I have set up abominations, and have multipled offences. Almighty Lord forgive me my sins. Now therefore I bow the knee of mine heart, beseeching thee of grace. Almighty Lord forgive me my sins. I have sinned, O Lord, I have sinned, and I acknowledge mine iniquities: wherefore, I humbly beseech thee, forgive me, O Lord, forgive me, and destroy me not with mine iniquities. Almighty Lord forgive me my sins. Be not angry with me for ever, by reserving evil for me; neither condemn me into the lower parts of the earth. Almighty Lord forgive me my sins. For thou art the God, even the God of them that repent; and in me thou wilt show all thy goodness: for thou wilt save me, that am unworthy, according to thy great mercy. Almighty Lord forgive me my sins. Therefore I will praise thee for ever all the days of my life: for all the powers of the heavens do praise thee, and thine is the glory for ever and ever. Almighty Lord forgive me my sins. Glory to the Father, &c. Amen.

Hymn of St. Mesrope (repeated thrice).

I BESEECH thee, O Lord, forgive me my sins. O merciful Lord have mercy upon me. God, be merciful to me a sinner. O God, my creator and my hope, have mercy upon me, thy sinful servant. Have mercy upon me a great sinner. O Holy and all-blessed and ever Virgin Mary, Mother of God, intercede for me a sinner. All ye saints of God intercede with the Father in heaven for us sinners. O Christ Son of God, most Benevolent, accept our supplications, for in thee do we put our trust. By the triumphal conquering power of thy Holy precious and life-giving Cross. protect us. Send, O Lord, the angel of peace, who coming may keep us in tranquility day and night. By thy benevolence, remember us, O Lord, remember us when thou comest with thy kingdom, and have mercy upon us.

―o―

Exhortation by the Deacon.
Prayer by the Priest.

―o―

Anthem.

PURGE me with hyssop, and I shall be clean : Wash me, and I shall be whiter than snow.

Have mercy upon me, O God, according to thy loving kindness : according unto the multitude of thy tender mercies blot out my transgressions. Wash me thoroughly from mine iniquity, and cleanse me from my sin. For I acknowledge my transgressions: and my sin is ever before me. Against thee, thee only, have I sinned, and done this evil in thy sight: that thou mightest be justified when thou speakest, and be clear when thou judgest. Behold, I was shapen in iniquity; and in sin did my mother conceive me. Behold, thou desirest truth in the inward parts, and in the hidden part thou shalt make me to know wisdom. Purge me with hyssop, and I shall be clean: wash me, and I shall be whiter than snow. Make me to hear joy and gladness, that the bones which thou hast broken may rejoice. Hide thy face from my sins, and blot out all mine iniquities. Create in me a clean heart, O God; and renew a right spirit within me. Cast me not away from thy presence; and take not thy holy spirit from me. Restore unto me the joy of thy salvation; and uphold me with thy free spirit. Then will I teach transgressors thy ways; and sinners shall be converted unto thee. Deliver me from blood guiltiness, O God, thou God of my salvation: and my tongue shall sing aloud of thy righteousness. O Lord, open thou my lips; and my mouth shall shew forth thy praise. For thou desirest not sacrifice, else would I give it: thou delightest not in burnt offering. The sacrifices of God are a broken spirit: a broken and a contrite heart, O God, thou wilt not despise. Do good in thy good pleasure unto Zion: build thou the walls of Jerusalem. Then shalt thou be pleased with the sacrifices of righteousness, with burnt offering and whole burnt offering: then shall they offer bullocks upon thine altar.—*Psalm, li, 1—19.*

Isaiah, lx, 20—22.

AND the days of thy mourning shall be ended; thy people also shall be all righteous: they shall inherit the land for ever, the branch of my planting, the work of my hands, that I may be glorified. A little one shall become a thousand, and a small one a strong nation: I, the Lord will hasten it in his time.

Ezekiel, xxxvi, 24—31.

FOR I will take you from among the heathen, and gather you out of all countries, and will bring you into your own land. Then will I sprinkle clean water upon you, and ye shall be clean from all your filthiness: and from all your idols will I cleanse you.

A new heart also will I give you, and a new spirit will I put within you: and I will take away the stony heart out of your flesh, and I will give you an heart of flesh. And I will put my spirit within you, and cause you to walk in my statutes, and ye shall keep my judgments, and do them. And ye shall dwell in the land that I gave to your fathers; and ye shall be my people, and I will be your God. I will also save you from all your uncleannesses: and I will call for the corn, and will increase it, and lay no famine upon you. And I will multiply the fruit of the tree, and the increase of the field, that ye shall receive no more reproach of famine among the heathen. Then shall ye remember your own evil days, and your doings that were not good, and shall loathe yourselves in your own sight for your iniquities and for your abominations.

Hebrews, x, 19—31.

HAVING therefore, brethren, boldness to enter into the holiest by the blood of Jesus, by a new and living way, which he hath consecrated for us, through the veil, that is to say, his flesh, and having an high priest over the house of God, let us draw near with a true heart in full assurance of faith, having our hearts sprinkled from an evil conscience, and our bodies washed with pure water. Let us hold fast the profession of our faith without wavering (for he is faithful that promised); and let us consider one another to provoke unto love and to good works: not forsaking the assembling of ourselves together, as the manner of some is; but exhorting one another: and so much the more, as ye see the day approaching. For if we sin wilfully after that we have received the knowledge of the truth, there remaineth no more sacrifice for sins; but a certain fearful looking for judgment and fiery indignation, which shall devour the adversaries. He that despised Moses' law died without mercy under two or three witnesses. Of how much sorer punishment, suppose ye, shall he be thought worthy, who hath trodden under foot the Son of God, and hath counted the blood of the covenant, wherewith he was sanctified, an unholy thing, and hath done despite unto the spirit of grace. For we know him that hath said, Vengeance belongeth unto me: I will recompense, said the Lord; and again: The Lord shall judge his people. It is a fearful thing to fall into the hands of the living God.

Psalm, xlii, 1. As the hart panteth after the waterbrooks, so panteth my soul after Thee O God.

St. Luke, vii, 36—50.

AND one of the Pharisees desired him that he would eat with him. And he went into the Pharisee's house, and sat down to meat. And, behold, a woman in the city, which was a sinner, when she knew that Jesus sat at meat in the Pharisee's house, brought an alabaster box of ointment, and stood at his feet behind him weeping, and began to wash his feet with tears, and did wipe them with the hairs of her head, and kissed his feet and anointed them with the ointment, Now when the Pharisee which had bidden him saw it he spoke within himself, saying, This man, if he were a prophet, would have known who and what manner of woman this is that toucheth him: for she is a sinner.

And Jesus answering said unto him, Simon, I have somewhat to say unto thee. And he said, Master, say on. There was a certain creditor which had two debtors: the one owed five hundred pence, and the other fifty. And when they had nothing to pay, he frankly forgave them both. Tell me, therefore, which of them will love him most? Simon answered and said, I suppose that he to whom he forgave most. And he said unto him, Thou hast rightly judged. And he turned to the woman, and said unto Simon, Seest thou this woman? I entered into thine house, thou gavest me no water for my feet: but she hath washed my feet with tears, and wiped them with the hair of her head. Thou gavest me no kiss: but this woman since the time I came in hath not ceased to kiss my feet. My head with oil thou didst not anoint: but this woman hath anointed my feet with ointment. Wherefore I say unto thee, Her sins, which are many, are forgiven; for she loved much: but to whom little is forgiven, the same loveth little. And he said unto her, Thy sins are forgiven. And they that sat at meat with him began to say within themselves, Who is this that forgiveth sins also? And he said to the woman, Thy faith hath saved thee; go in peace.

Exhortation by the Deacon.
Prayer of St. Basil.

Psalm, cxviii, 1—19.

O GIVE thanks unto the Lord; for he is good: because his mercy endureth for ever. Let Israel now say, that his mercy endureth for ever. Let the house of Aaron now say, that his mercy endureth for ever. Let them now that fear the Lord say, that his mercy endureth for ever. I called upon the Lord in distress: the Lord answered me, and set me in a large place. The Lord is on my side; I will not fear what can man do unto me? The Lord taketh my part with them that help me: therefore shall I see my desire upon them that hate me. It is better to trust in the Lord than to put confidence in man. It is better to trust in the Lord than to put confidence in princes. All nations compassed me about: but in the name of the Lord will I destroy them. They compassed me about; yea, they compassed me about: but in the name of the Lord I will destroy them. They compassed me about like bees; they are quenched as the fire of thorns: for in the name of the Lord I will destroy them. Thou hast thrust sore at me that I might fall: but the Lord helped me. The Lord is my strength and song, and is become my salvation. The voice of rejoicing and salvation is in the tabernacles of the righteous: the right hand of the Lord doeth valiantly. The right hand of the Lord is exalted: the right hand of the Lord doeth valiantly. I shall not die, but live, and declare the

HOLY THURSDAY MIDDAY.

works of the Lord. The Lord hath chastened me sore: but he hath not given me over unto death. Open to me the gates of righteousness: I will go into them, and I will praise the Lord.

Hymn of St. Peter.

Psalm, c, 1—5.

MAKE a joyful noise unto the Lord, all ye lands. Serve the Lord with gladness: come before his presence with singing. Know ye that the Lord he is God: it is he that hath made us, and not we ourselves; we are his people, and the sheep of his pasture. Enter into his gates with thanksgiving, and into his courts with praise: be thankful unto him, and bless his name. For the Lord is good; his mercy is everlasting; and his truth endureth to all generations.

Exhortation by the Deacon.
Prayer by the Priest.

The Bishop or a Priest will then read blessings upon the penitents.

Exhortation by the Deacon.
Litany.
Prayer by the Priest.

Service at Noon.

—o—

"OUR FATHER."

Psalm, li, 1—19.

"*Have mercy upon me, O God,*" *followed by Hymn.*
Prayers by the Priest.
Exhortations by the Deacon, and Psalms (see page 53).

"OUR FATHER."

Psalm, lxxxvi, 1—17.

"*Bow down thine ear, O Lord.*"
(The Prayers to follow here, see page 98).

—o—

Anthem.

I WILL wash mine hands in innocency: so will I compass thine altar, O Lord: Lord I have loved the habitation of thy house, and the place where thine honour dwelleth.—*Psalm, xxvi, 6, 8.*

Genesis, xxii, 1—18.

AND it came to pass after these things that God did tempt Abraham, and said unto him, Abraham; and he said, Behold, here I am. And he said, Take now thy son, thine only son Isaac, whom thou lovest, and get thee into the land of Moriah; and offer him there for a burnt offering upon one of the mountains which I will tell thee of. And Abraham rose up early in the morning, and saddled his ass, and took two of his young men with him, and Isaac his son, and clave the wood for the burnt offering, and rose up, and went unto the place of which God had told him. Then on the third day Abraham lifted up his eyes, and saw the place afar off. And Abraham said unto his young men, Abide ye here with the ass; and I and the lad will go yonder and worship, and come again to you. And Abraham took the wood of the burnt offering, and laid it upon Isaac his son; and he took the fire in his hand, and a knife; and they went both of them together. And Isaac spake unto Abraham his father, and said, My father; and he said, Here am I, my son. And he said, Behold the fire and the wood: but where is the lamb for a burnt offering? And Abraham said, My son, God will provide himself a lamb for a burnt offering: so they went both of them together. And they came to the place which God had told him of; and Abraham built an altar there, and laid the wood in order, and bound Isaac his son, and laid him on the altar upon the wood. And Abraham stretched forth his hand, and took the knife to slay his son. And the angel of the Lord called unto him out of heaven, and said, Abraham, Abraham; and he said, Here am I. And he said, Lay not thine hand upon the lad, neither do thou anything unto him: for now I know that thou fearest God, seeing thou hast not withheld thy son, thine only son from me. And Abraham lifted up his eyes, and looked, and behold, behind him a ram caught in a thicket by his horns: and Abraham went and took the ram, and offered him up for a burnt offering in the stead of his son. And Abraham called the name of that place Jehovah—jireh : as it is said to this day, In the mount of the Lord it shall be seen And the angel of the Lord called unto Abraham out of heaven the second time, and said, By myself have I sworn, saith the Lord, for because thou hast done this thing, and hast not withheld thy son, thine only son. That in blessing I will bless thee, and in multiplying I will multiply thy seed as the stars of the heaven, and as the sand which is upon the sea shore ; and thy seed shall possess the gate of his enemies ; and in thy seed shall all the nations of the earth be blessed, because thou hast obeyed my voice.

Isaiah, lxi, 1—7.

THE spirit of the Lord is upon me, because the Lord hath anointed me to preach good tidings unto the meek ; he hath sent me to bind up the broken-hearted, to proclaim liberty to the captives, and the opening of the prison to them that are bound ; to proclaim the acceptable year of the Lord, and the day of vengeance of our God ; to comfort all that mourn ; to appoint unto them that mourn in Zion ; to give unto them beauty for ashes, the oil of joy for mourning, the garment of praise for the spirit of heaviness; that they might be called trees of righteousness, the planting of the Lord, that he might be glorified. And they shall build the old wastes, they shall raise up the former desolations, and they shall repair the waste cities, the desolations of many generations. And strangers shall stand and feed your flocks, and the sons of the alien shall be your ploughmen and your vinedressers. But ye shall be named the Priests of the Lord, men shall call you the ministers of our God, ye shall eat the riches of the Gentiles, and in their glory shall ye boast yourselves. For your shame ye shall have double; and for confusion they shall rejoce in their portion: therefore in their land they shall possess the double: everlasting joy shall be unto them.

The Acts, i, 15—26.

AND in those days Peter stood up in the midst of the disciples and said (the number of names together were about an hundred and twenty), Men and brethren this scripture must needs have been fulfilled, which the Holy Ghost by the mouth of David spoke before concerning Judas, which was guide to them that took Jesus. For he was numbered with us, and had obtained part of this ministry. Now this man purchased a field with the reward of iniquity; and falling headlong, he burst asunder in the midst, and all his bowels gushed out. And it was known with all the dwellers at Jerusalem; inasmuch as that field is called in their proper tongue, Akeldama, that is to say, The field of blood. For it is written in the book of Psalms, Let his habitation be desolate, and let no man dwell therein: and his bishoprick let another take. Wherefore of these men which have companied with us all the time that the Lord Jesus went in and out among us, beginning from the baptism of John, unto that same day that he was taken up from us, must one be ordained to be a witness with us of his resurrection. And they appointed two, Joseph called Barsabas, who was surnamed Justus, and Matthias. And they prayed, and said, Thou, Lord, which knowest the hearts of all men, shew whether of these two thou hast chosen, that he may take part of this ministry and apostleship, from which Judas by transgression fell, that he might go to his own place. And they gave forth their lots; and the lot fell upon Matthias; and he was numbered with the eleven apostles.

―――o―――

Anthem.

HIS words were softer than oil: Yet were they drawn swords.

Give ear to my prayer, O God; and hide not thyself from my supplications. Attend unto me, and hear me: I mourn in my complaint, and make a noise; because of the voice of the enemy, because

HOLY THURSDAY MIDDAY.

of the oppression of the wicked: for they cast iniquity upon me, and in wrath they hate me. My heart is sore pained within me, and the terrors of death are fallen upon me. Fearfulness and trembling are come upon me, and horror hath overwhelmed me. And I said, Oh that I had wings like a dove! for then would I fly away, and be at rest, so then would I wander far off, and remain in the wilderness. I would hasten my escape from the windy storm and tempest. Destroy, O Lord, and divide their tongues; for I have seen violence and strife in the city. Day and night they go about it upon the walls thereof: mischief also and sorrow are in the midst of it. Wickedness is in the midst thereof: deceit and guile depart not from her streets. For it was not an enemy that reproached me; then I could have borne it: neither was it he that hated me that did magnify himself against me; then I would have hid myself from him: but it was thou, a man mine equal, my guide, and mine acquaintance. We took sweet council together, and walked unto the house of God in company. Let death seize upon them, and let them go down quick into hell: for wickedness is in their dwelling, and among them. As for me, I will call upon God; and the Lord shall save me. Evening and morning, and at noon, will I pray, and cry aloud: and he shall hear my voice. He hath delivered my soul in peace from the battle that was against me: for there were many with me. God shall hear, and afflict them, even he that abideth of old; because they have no changes, therefore they fear not God. He hath put forth his hands against such as be at peace with him : he hath broken his covenant. The words of his mouth were smoother than butter, but war was in his heart : his words were softer than oil, yet were they drawn swords. Cast thy burden upon the Lord, and he shall sustain thee : he shall never suffer the righteous to be moved. But thou, O God, shalt bring them down into the pit of destruction : bloody and deceitful men shall not live out half their days ; but I will trust in thee.—*Psalm, lv,* 1—23.

St. Mark, xiv, 1—26.

AFTER two days was the feast of the passover, and of unleavened bread : and the chief priests and the scribes sought how they might take him by craft, and put him to death. But they said, Not on the feast day, lest there be an uproar of the people. And being in Bethany in the house of Simon, the leper, as he sat at meat, there came a woman having an alabaster box of ointment of spikenard very precious ; and she brake the box, and poured it on his head. And there were some that had indignation within themselves, and said, Why was this waste of the ointment made ? For it might have been sold for more than three hundred pence, and have been given to the poor. And they murmured against her. And Jesus said, Let her alone; why trouble ye her? She hath wrought a good work on me. For ye have the poor with you always, and whensoever ye will ye may do them good: but me ye have not always. She hath done what she could: she is come aforehand to anoint my body to the burying. Verily I say unto you, Wheresoever this gospel shall be preached throughout the whole world, this also that she hath done shall be spoken of for a memorial of her. And Judas Iscariot, one of the twelve, went unto the chief priests, to betray him unto them. And when they heard it, they were glad, and promised to give him money. And he sought how he might conveniently betray him. And the first day of unleavened bread when they killed the passover, his disciples said unto him, Where wilt thou that we go and prepare that thou mayest eat the passover? And he sendeth forth two of his disciples, and saith unto them, Go ye into the city, and there shall meet you a man bearing a pitcher of water: follow him. And wheresoever he shall go in, say ye to the good man of the house, The Master saith, Where is the guest chamber where I shall eat the passover with my disciples? And he will shew you a large upper room furnished and prepared: there make ready for us. And his disciples went forth, and came into the city, and found as he had said unto them: and they made ready the passover. And in the evening he cometh with the twelve. And as they sat and did eat, Jesus said, Verily I say unto you, one of you which eateth with me shall betray me. And they began to be sorrowful, and to say unto him one by one, Is it I? and another said, Is it I? And he answered and said unto them, It is one of the twelve that dippeth with me in the dish. The Son of man indeed goeth, as it is written of him : but woe to that man by whom the Son of man is betrayed; good were it for that man if he had never been born. And as they did eat, Jesus took bread, and blessed, and break it, and gave to them, and said, TAKE, EAT: THIS IS MY BODY. And he took the cup, and when he had given thanks, he gave it to them : and they all drank of it. And he said unto them, THIS IS MY BLOOD of the new testament, which is shed for many. Verily I say unto you, I will drink no more of the fruit of the vine until that day that I drink it new in the kingdom of God. And when they had sung an hymn, they went out into the Mount of Olives. *While reading the Gospel the celebrant Priest will go up to the altar to begin the service of the Holy Mass.*

———o———

Litany by the Deacon.
Trisagion.
Hymn of St. Isaac.
Exhortation by the Deacon.
Prayer by the Priest.

———o———

Anthem.

Thou preparest a table before me in the presence of mine enemies.

THE Lord is my shepherd; I shall not want. He maketh me to lie down in green pastures: he leadeth me beside the still waters. He restoreth my soul: he leadeth me in the paths of righteousness for his name's sake. Yea, though I walk through the valley of the shadow of death, I will fear no evil: for thou art with me; thy rod and thy staff they comfort me Thou preparest a table before me in the presence of mine enemies: thou anointest my head with oil; my cup runneth over. Surely goodness and mercy shall follow me all the days of my life: and I will dwell in the house of the Lord for ever.—*Psalm, xxiii*, 1—6. *I Corinthians, xi*, 23—32.

FOR I have received of the Lord that which also I delivered unto you, that the Lord Jesus the same night in which he was betrayed took bread. And when he had given thanks he break it, and said, Take, eat: this is my body, which is broken for you: this do in remembrance of me. After the same manner also he took the cup, when he had supped, saying, This cup is a new testament in my blood: this do ye, as oft, as you drink it, in remembrance of me. For as often as ye eat this bread, and drink this cup, ye do shew the Lord's death till he come. Wherefore whosoever shall eat this bread, and drink this cup of the

Lord, unworthily, shall be guilty of the body and blood of the Lord. But let a man examine himself, and so let him eat of that bread and drink of that cup. For he that eateth and drinketh unworthily, eateth and drinketh damnation to himself, not discerning the Lord's body. For this cause many are weak and sickly among you, and many sleep. For if we would judge ourselves, we should not be judged. But when we are judged, we are chastened of the Lord, that we should not be condemned with the world.

St. Matthew, 17—30.

NOW the first day of the feast of unleavened bread the disciples came to Jesus, saying unto him, Where wilt thou that we prepare for thee to eat the passover? And he said, Go into the city to such a man, and say unto him, The Master saith, My time is at hand; I will keep the passover at thy house with my disciples. And the disciples did as Jesus had appointed them; and they made ready the passover. Now when the even was come, he sat down with the twelve. And as they did eat, he said, Verily I say unto you, that one of you shall betray me. And they were exceeding sorrowful, and began every one of them to say unto him, Lord, is it I? And he answered and said, He that dippeth his hand with me in the dish, the same shall betray me. The Son of man goeth as it is written of him, but woe unto that man by whom the Son of man is betrayed!

HOLY THURSDAY MIDDAY. 51

It had been good for that man if he had not been born. Then Judas, which betrayed him, answered and said, Master, is it I! He said unto him, Thou hast said. And as they were eating, Jesus took bread, and blessed it, and break it, and gave it to the disciples, and said, TAKE, EAT; THIS IS MY BODY. And he took the cup, and gave thanks, and gave it to them, saying, DRINK YE ALL OF IT. FOR THIS IS MY BLOOD of the new testament which is shed for many for the remission of sins. But I say unto you, I will not drink henceforth of this fruit of the vine, until that day when I drink it new with you in my Father's kingdom. And when they had sung an hymn, they went out into the Mount of Olives.

Then they will draw the curtain, and say the Nicene Creed.

WE BELIEVE in one God the Father Almighty, Maker of Heaven and Earth, and of all things visible and invisible: And we believe in one Lord Jesus Christ, the Only Begotten Son of God, begotten of His Father, of the very essence of the Father, God of God, Light of Light, Very God of very God Begotten not made, being of one substance with the Father, by Whom all things were made, in heaven and in earth, visible and invisible: Who for us men and for our salvation came down from heaven, was incarnate, and was made man and perfectly begotten by the Holy Ghost of the Most Holy Virgin Mary. He assumed from her flesh, soul, and mind, and all things that are in man, truly and not figuratively: He suffered, was crucified and buried, and the third day He rose again, and ascended into heaven with the same Body, and sitteth on the right hand of the Father, and He shall come with the same Body, and in the glory of His Father, to judge both the quick and the dead. Whose kingdom shall have no end. We also believe in the Holy Ghost not created, most perfect. Who spake in the Law, in the Prophets, and in the Gospels. Who descended upon Jordan. Who preached Him that was sent! Who dwelleth in the Saints. We also believe One only Catholic and Apostolic Church. One Baptism to repentance, for the remission of sins. The resurrection of the dead, the eternal judgment both of souls and bodies. the kingdom of heaven, and the life everlasting: And for them that say, There was a time when the Son of God was not, or, in like manner, There was a time when the Holy Ghost was not, or, that they were made of nothing, or that the Son of God and the Holy Ghost are of another substance, or that they are mutable, the Orthodox and Apostolic Church saith, Let them be anathema.

Confession of St. Gregory.

AND we also glorify Him Who was before all worlds! We worship the Holy Trinity, and the One

Godhead, Father, Son, and Holy Ghost, now and for ever, and to all ages. Amen.

During the Service of the Holy Mass at the time of " Lord's Prayer" the Bishop or a Priest with the Holy Cross and the Gospel in his hand will read from the altar the Words of admonition and exhortation of St. Basil to the people concerning the Blessed Sacrament.

HOLY THURSDAY EVENING.

Ceremony of Washing of Feet.

Anthem.

PURGE me with hyssop, and I shall be clean: Wash me, and I shall be whiter than snow.

HAVE mercy upon me, O God, according to thy loving kindness: according unto the multitude of thy tender mercies blot out my transgressions. Wash me throughly from mine iniquity, and cleanse me from my sin. For I acknowledge my transgressions, and my sin is ever before me. Against thee, thee only, have I sinned, and done this evil in thy sight: that thou mightest be justified when thou speakest, and be clear when thou judgest. Behold, I was shapen in iniquity; and in sin did my mother conceive me. Behold, thou desirest truth in the inward parts: and in the hidden part thou shalt make me to know wisdom. Purge me with hyssop, and I shall be clean; wash me, and I shall be whiter than snow. Make me to hear joy and gladness, that the bones which thou hast broken may rejoice. Hide thy face from my sins, and blot out all mine iniquities. Create in me a clear heart, O God; and renew a right spirit within me. Cast me not away from thy presence; and take not thy holy spirit from me. Restore unto me the joy of thy salvation; and uphold me with thy free spirit. Then will I teach transgressors thy ways; and sinners shall be converted unto thee. Deliver me from blood guiltiness, O God, thou God of my salvation: and my tongue shall sing aloud of thy righteousness. O Lord, open thou my lips; and my mouth shall shew forth thy praise. For thou desirest not sacrifice; else would I give it: thou delightest not in burnt offerings. The sacrifices of God are a broken spirit: a broken and a contrite heart, O God, thou wilt not despise. Do good in thy good pleasure unto Zion: build thou the walls of Jerusalem. Then shalt thou be pleased with the sacrifices of righteousness, with burnt offering and whole burnt offering: then shall they offer bullocks upon thine altar.—*Psalm, li,* 1—19.

Hymn of St. Isaac.
Exhortation by the Deacon.
Litany.
Prayer by the Priest.

Here, pouring water into the Basin, the following Psalm will be said:—

Psalm, xxix, 1—11.

" The voice of the Lord is upon waters, etc."

GIVE unto the Lord, O ye mighty, give unto the Lord glory and strength. Give unto the Lord the glory due unto his name; worship the Lord in the beauty of holiness. The voice of the Lord is upon the waters: the God of glory thundereth: the Lord is upon many waters. The voice of the Lord is powerful; the voice of the Lord is full of majesty. The voice of the Lord breaketh the cedars; yea, the Lord breaketh the cedars of Lebanon. He maketh them also to skip like a calf; Lebanon and Sirion like a young unicorn. The voice of the Lord divideth the flames of fire. The voice of the Lord shaketh the wilderness; the Lord shaketh the wilderness of Kadesh. The voice of the Lord maketh the hinds to calve, and discovereth the forests; and in his temple doth every one speak of his glory. The Lord sitteth upon the floods; yea, the Lord sitteth King for ever. The Lord will give strength unto his people; the Lord will bless his people with peace.

Exodus, xxx, 17—21.

AND the Lord spake unto Moses, saying, Thou shalt also make a laver of brass, and his foot also of brass, to wash withal: and thou shalt put it between the tabernacle of the congregation and the altar, and thou shalt put water therein. For Aaron and his sons shall wash their hands and their feet thereat. When they go into the tabernacle of the congregation, they shall wash with water, that they die not; or when they come near to the altar to minister, to burn offering made by fire unto the Lord. So they shall wash their hands and their feet, that they die not: and it shall be a statute for ever to them, even to him and to his seed throughout their generations.

I Kings, vii, 38—40.

THEN made he ten lavers of brass: one laver contained forty baths: and every laver was four cubits; and upon every one of the ten bases one laver. And he put five bases on the right side of the house, and five on the left side of the house, and he set the sea on the right side of the house eastward over against the south. And Hiram made the lavers, and the shovels, and the basons; so Hiram made an end of doing all the work that he made King Solomon for the house of the Lord.

II Chronicles, iv, 2—6.

ALSO he made a molten sea of ten cubits from brim to brim, round in compass, and five cubits the height thereof; and a line of thirty cubits did compass it round about. And under it was the similitude of oxen, which did compass it round about: ten in a cubit, compassing the sea round about. Two rows of oxen were cast, when it was cast. It stood upon twelve oxen, three looking toward north, and three looking toward the west, and three looking toward the south, and three looking toward the east, and the sea was set above upon them, and all their hinder parts were inward. And the thickness of it was an hand breadth, and the brim of it like the word of the brim of a cup, with flowers of lilies; and it received and held three thousand baths. He made also ten lavers, and put five on the right hand, and five on the left, to wash in them: such things as they offered for the burnt offering they washed in them; but the sea was for the priests to wash in.

Isaiah, xliv, 2—6.

FEAR not, O Jacob, my servant; and thou Jesurun, whom I have chosen. For I will pour water upon him that is thirsty, and floods upon the dry ground: I will pour my spirit upon thy seed, and my blessing upon thine offspring. And they shall spring up as among the grass, as willows by the water courses. One shall say, I am the Lord's; and another shall call himself by the name of Jacob; and another shall subscribe with his hand unto the Lord, and surname himself by the name of Israel. Thus saith the Lord the King of Israel, and his redeemer the Lord of hosts, I am the first, and I am the last; and beside me there is no God.

I Corinthians, x, 1—4.

MOREOVER, brethren, I would not that ye should be ignorant, how that all our fathers were under the cloud, and all passed through the sea: and were all baptized unto Moses in the cloud and in the sea; and did all eat the same spiritual meat; and did all drink the same spiritual drink: for they drank of that spiritual Rock that followed them: and that Rock was Christ.

I John, iv, 7—21.

BELOVED, let us love one another: for love is of God; and every one that loveth is born of God, and knoweth God. He that loveth not knoweth not God; for God is love. In this was manifested the love of God towards us, because that God sent his only begotten Son into the world, that we might live through him. Herein is love, not that we loved God, but that he loved us, and sent his Son to be the propitiation for our sins. Beloved, if God so loved us, we ought also to love one another. No man hath seen God at any time. If we love one another, God dwelleth in us, and his love is perfected in us. Hereby know we that we dwell in him, and he in us, because he hath given us of his spirit. And we have seen and do testify that the Father sent the Son to be the Saviour of the world. Whosoever shall confess that Jesus is the Son of God, God dwelleth in him, and he in God. And we have known and believed the love that God hath to us, God is love ; and he that dwelleth in love dwelleth in God, and God in him. Herein is our love made perfect, that we may have boldness in the day of judgment ; because as he is, so are we in this world. There is no fear in love ; but perfect love casteth out fear : because fear hath torment. He that feareth is not made perfect in love. We love him, because he first loved us. If a man say, I love God, and hateth his brother, he is a liar ; for he that loveth not his brother whom he hath seen, how can he love God whom he hath not seen ? And this commandment have we from him, That he who loveth God love his brother also.

Prayers of St. JOHN (Bishop) on Love.

St. John, xiii, 1—11.

NOW, before the feast of the passover, when Jesus knew that his hour was come that he should depart out of this world unto the Father. having loved his own which were in the world, he loved them unto the end. And supper being ended, the devil having now put into the heart of Judas Iscariot, Simon's son, to betray him ; Jesus knowing that the Father had given all things into his hands, and that he was come from

God, and went to God; He riseth from supper, and laid aside his garments; and took a towel, and girded himself. After that he poureth water into a bason, and began to wash the disciples' feet, and to wipe them with the towel wherewith he was girded. Then cometh he to Simon Peter: and Peter saith unto him, Lord, dost thou wash my feet? Jesus answered and said unto him, What I do thou knowest not now; but thou shalt know hereafter. Peter saith unto him, Thou shalt never wash my feet. Jesus answered him, If I wash thee not, thou hast no part with me. Simon Peter saith unto him, Lord, not my feet only, but also my hands and my head. Jesus saith to him, He that is washed needeth not save to wash his feet, but is clean every whit: and ye are clean, but not all. For he knew who should betray him; therefore said he, Ye are not all clean.

---o---

Prayer by the Deacon.
Hymn of St. Arachel.
Prayer by the Priest on the oil and water.
Then the oil and the water will be blessed by the Cross and the Holy Gospel.

Prayer by the Deacon.
Prayer by the Priests.
Hymn of St. Isaac.

---o---

(Here the washing of feet begins.)
Hymn of St. Nierses the Graceful.

I.

THIS day the Origin of Light Ineffable, for the completion of our salvation, entered the Upper-room to celebrate the last of the shadowy Feasts. Before the mystic supper, the Diffuser of Light girded Himself with an apron; and brought water, like a menial, to wash the feet of His disciples.

II.

When the Glorious Word of God approached Peter, that disciple refused his feet to those Hands that created the heaven and the earth; even to those Hands that restored sight to the blind; that healed the dumb and the deaf; that had lifted him from the sea and checked the waves, and they were calm.

III.

Then Our Lord rebuked the Chief of His small flock for not comprehending the mystery; and being convinced Peter implored that not only his feet but his head also should be washed: Our Lord replied, " You need not wash with water your Head,* which is already clean, but let your feet be washed that you may be united with me, your Head, in holiness."

IV.

This day our Lord by examples in His own person showed extreme humility to the body of his disciples, whom He had

---

* The word "Head" here refers to Our Blessed Lord, and the word "feet" to the whole body of the Apostles. The meaning of the passage, therefore, is :—" You need not wash with water your Lord, your Head.—He is clean, but let your feet—the whole company of the Apostles be washed, that you may be united with your Lord, your Head, in holiness."

taught before by precepts; the Unseen of the Angels serving the children of the earth, and the Adorned of the seraphim ministering to his servants.

V.

"If I, the Lord of the Creation, and your Master," said He, "by washing your feet, my servants and disciples, have cleansed your old sins, manifest ye, in like manner, towards each other the same humility, to the overthrow of the proud and to the lifting up of your fallen nature."

VI.

As Thou hast rendered Thy disciples pure by washing their feet with water with Thy holy Hands, and as Thou hast taught them to conquer pride by means of humility; Oh, do thou wash off the impurities of my sins through the supplication of Thy Holy Board, and direct my footsteps, that I may ascend to heaven through meekness.

VII.

He fulfilled the Laws that were delivered to Moses at Sinai; He ate the typical lamb and the unleavened bread with bitter herbs; changing the old into new rites; converting the shadow into light, and offering Himself instead of the lamb of the passover, as the Lamb of God.

VIII.

Instead of the unleavened bread He gave His own Divine Body—Virgin-born, immaculate, incorruptible. Instead of the blood of the sheep of the covenant, He offered His own Blood, as a new testament: instead of the bitterest endive He bequeathed as a substitute a pure and holy life.

IX.

The King of the Creation gave the Bread of Life to those who were hungry, and the Cup of Bliss to those who were afflicted as the children of Adam. "This is," said He, "the new covenant of My Blood, instead of the old covenant of blood, which he shall keep in remembrance of Me, until I return among you again."

X.

We, who have assembled together, beseech Thee, together with the congregated eleven, on whom Thou hast bestowed Thy redeeming body with the cup; grant to us also, Oh Lord! with them the liberty of partaking at Thy table of the Bread of Life, which we desire, and the drink we thirst for.

XI.

From the chosen disciples, the holy Lambs, Judas separated himself, and the Lamb of God, the Bearer of our sins, was betrayed unto death for silver. To the Divine Supper the audacious and the proud traitor approached, and by dining with his Master he increased his perfidy.

XII.

The light besought in a supplicating tone that the bewildred may be restored: "One of you, O Brethren!" said He, "shall betray Me unto death." And Peter was alarmed; and beckoning John, asked him to question, who was to betray their Master.

St. John, xiii, 12—15.

SO after he had washed their feet, and had taken his garments, and was set down again, he said unto them, Know ye what I have done to you? Ye call me Master and Lord: and ye say well, for so I am, If I then, your Lord and Master, have washed your feet, ye also ought to wash one another's feet. For I have given you an example, that ye should do as I have done to you.

—o—

Prayer by the Deacon.
Prayer by the Priest.
"OUR FATHER."

HOLY THURSDAY. NIGHT SERVICE.

—o—

OUR FATHER. "O LORD, OPEN THOU MY LIPS; AND MY MOUTH SHALL SHEW FORTH THY PRAISE, ETC. *(repeated twice).*

—o—

Psalm, iii, 1—8.

LORD how are they increased that trouble me! many are they that rise up against me. Many there be which say of my soul, There is no help for him in God. But thou, O Lord, art a shield for me; my glory, and the lifter up of mine head. I cried unto the Lord with my voice, and he heard me out of his holy hill. I laid me down and slept; I awaked; for the Lord sustained me. I will not be afraid of ten thousands of people that have set themselves against me round about. Arise, O Lord; save me, O my God: for thou hast smitten all mine enemies upon the cheek bone; thou hast broken the teeth of the ungodly. Salvation belongeth unto the Lord; thy blessing is upon thy people.

Psalm, lxxxviii, 1—18.

O LORD God of my salvation, I have cried day and night before thee: let my prayer come before thee: incline thine ear unto my cry; for my soul is full of troubles: and my life draweth nigh unto the grave. I am counted with them that go down into the pit: I am as a man that hath no strength: free among the death, like the slain that lie in the grave, whom thou rememberest no more: and they are cut off from thy hand. Thou hast laid me in the lowest pit, in darkness, in the deeps. Thy wrath lieth hard upon me, and thou hast afflicted me with all thy waves. Thou hast put away mine acquaintance far from me; thou hast made me an abomination unto them; I am shut up, and I cannot come forth. Mine eye mourneth by reason of affliction: Lord, I have called daily upon thee; I have stretched out my hands unto thee. Wilt thou shew wonders to the dead? Shall the dead arise and praise thee? Shall thy loving kindness be declared in the grave? or thy faithfulness in destruction? Shall thy wonders be known in the dark? and thy righteousness in the land of forgetfulness? But unto thee have I cried, O Lord, and in the morning shall my prayer prevent thee. Lord, why castest thou off my soul? why hidest thou thy face from me? I am afflicted and ready to die from my youth up: while I suffer thy terrors I am distracted. Thy fierce wrath goeth over me; thy terrors have cut me off. They come round about me daily like water; they compassed me about together. Lover and friend hast thou put far from me, and mine acquaintance into darkness.

Psalm, ciii, 1—22.

BLESS the Lord, O my soul: and all that is within me, bless his holy name. Bless the Lord, O my soul, and forget not all his benefits: who forgiveth all thine iniquities; who healeth all thy diseases; who redeemeth thy life from destruction; who crowneth thee with loving kindness and tender mercies; who satisfieth thy mouth with good things; so that thy youth is renewed like the eagle's. The Lord executeth righteousness and judgment for all that are oppressed. He made known his ways unto Moses, his acts unto the children of Israel. The Lord is merciful and gracious, slow to anger, and plenteous in mercy. He will not always chide: neither will he keep his anger for ever. He hath not dealt with us after our sins; nor rewarded us according to our iniquities. For as the heaven is high above the earth, so great is his mercy toward them that fear him. As far as the east is from the west, so far hath he removed our transgressions from us. Like as a father pitieth his children, so the Lord pitieth them that fear him. For he knoweth our frame; he remembereth that we are dust. As for man, his days are as grass: as a flower of the field so he flourisheth. For the wind passeth over it, and it is gone; and the place thereof shall know it no more. But the mercy of the Lord is from everlasting to everlasting upon them that fear him; and his righteousness unto children's children: to such as keep his covenant, and to those that remember his commandments to do them. The Lord hath prepared his throne in the heavens; and his kingdom ruleth over all. Bless the Lord, ye his angels, that excel in strength, that do his commandments, hearkening unto the voice of his word. Bless ye the Lord, all ye his hosts; ye ministers of his, that do his pleasure. Bless the Lord, all his works in all places of his dominion: bless the Lord, O my soul.

Psalm, cxliii, 1—12.

HEAR my prayer, O Lord, give ear to my supplications: in thy faithfulness answer me, and in thy righteousness. And enter not into judgment with thy servant: for in thy sight shall no man living be justified. For the enemy hath persecuted my soul; he hath smitten my life down to the ground: he hath made me to dwell in darkness, as those that have been long dead Therefore is my spirit overwhelmed within me; my heart within me is desolate. I remember the days of old; I meditate on all thy works; I muse on the work of thy hands. I stretch forth my hands unto thee; my soul thirsted after thee, as a thristy land. Hear me speedily, O Lord: my spirit faileth: hide not thy face from me, lest I be like unto them that go down into the pit. Cause me to hear thy loving kindness in the morning; for in thee do I trust: cause me to know the way wherein I should walk; for I lift up my soul unto thee. Deliver me, O Lord, from mine enemies: I flee unto thee to hide me. Teach me to do thy will; for thou art my God: thy spirit is good; lead me into the land of uprightness. Quicken me, O Lord, for thy name's sake: for thy righteousness' sake bring my soul out of trouble. And of thy mercy cut off mine enemies and destroy all them that afflict my soul: for I am thy servant.

———o———

Hymns of St. Nierses the Graceful.
Litany.
Another Hymn of St. Nierses.
Prayer by the Priest.
" *We thank thee, O Lord our God.*"

Anthem.

(Psalms, cxlvi, cxlviii).

PRAISE ye the Lord. Praise the Lord, O my soul. While I live will I praise the Lord, Alleluia will sing praises unto my God while I have any being Alleluia. Put not your trust in princes, nor in the son of man in whom there is no help, Alleluia. His breath goeth forth, he returneth to his earth; in that very day his thoughts perish, Alleluia. Happy is he that hath the God of Jacob for his help, whose hope is in the Lord his God, Alleluia; which made heaven, and earth, the sea, and all that therein is: which keepeth truth for ever, Alleluia. Praise the Lord, O Jerusalem; praise thy God, O Zion, Alleluia, Alleluia. For he hath strengthened the bars of thy gates; he hath blessed thy children within thee, Alleluia, Alleluia. He maketh peace in thy borders, and filled thee with the finest of the wheat, Alleluia, Alleluia. He sendeth forth his commandment upon earth: his word runneth very swiftly, Alleluia, Alleluia. He giveth snow like wool; he scattereth the hoarfrost like ashes, Alleluia, Alleluia. He casteth forth his icelike morsels: who can stand before his cold? Alleluia, Alleluia. He sendeth out his word, and melted them: he causeth his wind to blow and the waters flow, Alleluia, Alleluia. He sheweth his word unto Jacob; his statutes and his judgments unto Israel, Alleluia, Alleluia. He hath not dealt so with any nation: and as for his judgments, they have not known them, Alleluia. Alleluia.

Hymn of St. Isaac.

Deacon: Let us pray to the Lord in peace.

Priest: Blessing and glory to the Father, and to the Son, and to the Holy Ghost, now and ever, world without end. Amen.

Psalm, ii, 1—12.

WHY do the heathen rage, and the people imagine a vain thing? The King of the earth set themselves, and the rulers take counsel together, against the Lord, and against his anointed, saying, Let us break their bonds asunder, and cast away their cords from us. He that sitteth in the heavens shall laugh: the Lord shall have them in derision. Then shall he break unto them in his wrath, and wax them in his sore displeasure. Yet have I set my King upon my holy hill of Zion. I will declare the decree; the Lord hath said unto me, Thou art my Son; this day have I begotten thee. Ask of me, and I shall give thee heathen for thine inheritance, and the uttermost parts of the earth for thy possession.

Thou shalt break them with a rod of iron; thou shalt dash them in pieces like a potter's vessel. Be wise now, therefore, O ye kings: be instructed, ye judges of the earth. Serve the Lord with fear and rejoice with trembling. Kiss the son, lest he be angry, and ye perish from the way, when his wrath is kindled but a little. Blessed are all they that put their trust in him.

Psalm, iii, 1—8.

LORD, how are they increased that trouble me many are they that rise up against me. Many there be which say of my soul, There is no help for him in God. But thou, O Lord, art a shield for me, my glory, and the lifter up of mine head. I cried unto the Lord with my voice, and he heard me out of his holy hill. I laid me down and slept; I awaked; for the Lord sustained me. I will not be afraid of ten thousands of people that have set themselves against me round about. Arise, O Lord; save me, O my God: for thou hast smitten all mine enemies upon the cheek bone; thou hast broken the teeth of the ungodly. Salvation belongeth unto the Lord: thy blessing is upon thy people.

Psalm, iv, 1—8.

HEAR me when I call, O God of my righteousness: thou hast enlarged me when I was in distress; have mercy upon me, and hear my prayer. O ye sons of men, how long will ye turn my glory into shame? how long will ye love vanity, and seek after leasing? But know that the Lord hath set apart him that is godly for himself: the Lord will hear when I call unto him. Stand in awe, and sin not: commune with your own heart upon your bed, and be still. Offer the sacrifices of righteousness, and put your trust in the Lord. There be many that say, Who will shew us any good? Lord, lift thou up the light of thy countenance upon us. Thou hast put gladness in my heart, more than in the time that their corn and their wine increased. I will both lay me down in peace, and sleep: for thou, *Lord*, *only* makest me dwell in safety.

Anthem.

THE rulers take counsel together against the Lord, and against his anointed (*repeated thrice*).—*Psalm ii, 2.*

Hymn of St. Nierses the Graceful on the Passions of our Saviour.

I

This day the Origin of Light Ineffable, for the completion of our salvation, entered the Upper-room to celebrate the last of the shadowy Feasts. Before the mystic supper, the Diffuser of Light girded Himself with an apron; and brought water, like a menial, to wash the feet of His disciples.

II.

When the Glorious Word of God approached Peter, that disciple refused his feet to those Hands that created the heaven and the earth ; even to those Hands that restored sight to the blind ; that healed the dumb and the deaf ; that had lifted him from the sea and checked the waves, and they were calm.

III.

Then Our Lord rebuked the Chief of His small flock for not comprehending the mystery ; and being convinced, Peter implored that not only his feet but his head* also should be washed : Our Lord replied, " You need not wash with water your Head, which is already clean, but let your feet be washed that you may be united with me, your Head, in holiness."

IV.

This day our Lord by examples in His own person showed extreme humility to the body of His disciples, whom He had taught before by precepts ; the Unseen of the Angels serving the children of the earth, and the Adorned of the seraphim ministering to his servants.

V.

" If I, the Lord of the Creation, and your Master," said He, " by washing your feet, my servants and disciples, have cleansed your old sins, manifest ye, in like manner, towards each other the same humility, to the overthrow of the proud and to the lifting up of your fallen nature."

---

* The word "Head" here refers to Our Blessed Lord, and the word "feet" to the whole body of the Apostles. The meaning of the passage, therefore, is :—" You need not wash with water your Lord, your Head,—He is clean, but let your feet,—the whole company of the Apostles be washed, that you may be united with your Lord, your Head, in holiness."

VI.

As Thou hast rendered Thy disciples pure by washing their feet with water with Thy holy Hands, and as Thou hast taught them to conquer pride by means of humility; Oh, do thou wash off the impurities of my sins through the supplication of Thy Holy Board, and direct my footsteps that I may ascend to heaven through meekness.

St. John, xiii, 16—xviii, 1.

VERILY, Verily, I say unto you, The servant is not greater than his Lord; neither he that is sent greater than he that sent him. If ye know these things, happy are ye if ye do them. I speak not of you all: I know whom I have chosen: but that the scripture may be fulfilled, He that eateth bread with me hath lifted up his heel against me. Now I tell you before it come, that, when it is come to pass, ye may believe that I am he. Verily, Verily, I say unto you, He that receiveth whomsoever I send receiveth me; and he that receiveth me receiveth him that sent me. When Jesus had thus said, he was troubled in spirit, and testified, and said, Verily verily, I say unto you, that one of you shall betray me. Then the disciples looked one on another doubting of whom he spake. Now there was leaning on Jesus' bosom one of his disciples, whom Jesus loved. Simon Peter therefore beckoned to him, that he should ask who it should be of whom he spake. He then lying on Jesus' breast, saith unto him, Lord, who is it? Jesus answered, He it is to whom I shall give a sop when I have dipped it. And when he had dipped the sop, he gave it to Judas Iscariot, the son of Simon. And after the sop Satan entered into him. Then said Jesus unto him, That thou doest, do quickly. Now no man at the table knew for what intent he spake this unto him. For some of them thought, because Judas had the bag, that Jesus had said unto him, Buy those things that one have need of against the feast; or, that he should give something to the poor. He then having received the sop went immediately out: and it was night. Therefore when he was gone out, Jesus said, Now is the Son of man glorified, and God is glorified in him. If God be glorified in him, God shall also glorify him in himself, and shall straightway glorify him. Little children, yet a little while I am with you. Ye shall seek me, and as I said unto the Jews, whither I go, ye cannot come; so now I say to you. A new commandment I give unto you, that ye love one another; as I have loved you, that ye also love one another. By this shall all men know that ye are my disciples, if ye have love one to another. Simon Peter said unto him, Lord, whither goest thou? Jesus answered him, Whither I go, thou canst not follow me now: but thou shalt follow me afterwards. Peter said unto him, Lord, why cannot I follow thee now? I will lay down my life for thy sake. Jesus answered him, Wilt thou lay down thy life for my sake? Verily, verily, I say unto thee, The cock shall not crow, till thou hast denied me thrice. Let not your heart be troubled: ye believe in God, believe also in me. In my Father's house are many mansions: if it were not so, I would have told you. I go to prepare a place for you. And if I go and prepare a place for you, I will come again, and receive you unto myself; that where I am, there ye may be also. And whither I go ye know, and the way ye know. Thomas saith unto him, Lord, we know not whither thou goest; and how can we know the way? Jesus saith unto him, I am the way, the truth, and the life: no man cometh unto the Father, but by me. If he had known me, ye should have known my Father also: and from henceforth ye know him, and have seen him. Philip saith unto him, Lord, shew us the Father, and it sufficeth us. Jesus saith unto him, Have I been so long time with you, and yet hast thou not known me, Philip? He that hath seen me hath seen the Father; and how sayest thou then, Shew us the Father? Believest thou not that I am in the Father, and the Father in me! The words that I speak unto you I speak not of myself: but the Father that dwelleth in me, he doeth the works, Believe me that I am in the Father, and the Father in me: or else believe me for the very work's sake. Verily, verily, I say unto you, He that believeth on me, the works that I do shall he do also; and greater works than these shall he do; because I go unto my Father. And whatsoever ye shall ask in my name, that will I do, that the Father may be glorified in the Son. If ye shall ask anything in my name, I will do it. If ye love me, keep my commandments. And I will pray the Father, and he shall give you another comforter that he may abide with you for ever; even the spirit of truth; whom the world cannot receive, because it seeth him not, neither knoweth him; but ye know him; for he dwelleth with you and shall be in you. I will not leave you comfortless: I will come to you. Yet a little while, and the world seeth me no more; but ye see me: because I live, ye shall live also. At that day ye shall know that I am in my Father, and ye in me, and I in you. He that hath my commandments, and keepeth them, he it is that loveth me; and he that loveth me shall be loved of my Father, and I will love him, and will manifest myself to him. Judas saith unto him, not Iscariot, Lord, how is it that thou wilt manifest thyself unto us, and not unto the world? Jesus answered and said unto him, If a man love me, he will keep my word: and my Father will love him, and we will come unto him, and make our abode with him. He that loveth me not keepeth not my sayings: and the word which ye hear is not mine, but the Father's which sent me.

These things have I spoken unto you, being yet present with you. But the Comforter, which is the Holy Ghost, whom the Father will send in my name, he shall teach you all things, and bring all things to your remembrance, whatsoever I have said unto you. Peace I leave with you, my peace I will give unto you: not as the world giveth, give I unto you. Let not your heart be troubled, neither let it be afraid. Ye have heard how I said unto you, I go away, and come again unto you. If ye loved me, ye would rejoice, because I said, I go unto the Father: for my Father is greater than I. And now I have told you before it come to pass, that, when it is come to pass, ye might believe. Hereafter I will not talk much with you: for the prince of this world cometh, and hath nothing in me. But that the world may know that I love the Father; and as the Father gave me commandment, even as I do. Arise, let us go hence. I am the true vine, and my Father is the husbandman. Every branch in me that beareth not fruit he taketh away: and every branch that beareth fruit, he purgeth it, that it may bring forth more fruit. Now ye are clean through the word which I have spoken unto you. Abide in me, and I in you. As the branch cannot bear fruit of itself, except it abide in the vine, no more can ye, except ye abide in me. I am the vine, ye are the branches: he that abideth in me, and I in him, the same bringeth forth much fruit: for without me ye can do nothing. If a man abide not in me, he is cast forth as a branch, and is withered; and men gather them, and cast them into the fire, and they are burned. If ye abide in me, and my words abide in you, ye shall ask what ye will, and it shall be done unto you. Herein is my Father glorified, that ye bear much fruit; so shall ye be my disciples. As the Father hath loved me, so have I loved you: continue ye in my love. If ye keep my commandments, ye shall abide in my love; even as I have kept my Father's commandments, and abide in his love. These things have I spoken unto you, that my joy might remain in you, and that your joy might be full. This is my commandment, that ye love one another, as I have loved you. Greater love hath no man than this, that a man lay down his life for his friends. Ye are my friends, if ye do whatsoever I command you. Henceforth I call you not servants; for the servant knoweth not what his Lord doeth: but I have called you friends: for all things that I have heard of my Father I have made known unto you. Ye have not chosen me, but I have chosen you, and ordained you, that ye should go and bring forth fruit, and that your fruit should remain: that whatsoever ye shall ask of the Father in my name, he may give it you. These things I command you, that ye love one another. If the world hate you, ye know that it hated me before it hated you. If ye were of the world, the world would love his own: but because ye are not of the world, but

I have chosen you out of the world, therefore the world hateth you. Remember the word that I said unto you, The servant is not greater than his Lord. If they have persecuted me, they will also persecute you; if they have kept my saying, they will keep your's also. But all these things will they do unto you for my name's sake, because they know not him that sent me. If I had not come and spoken unto them, they had not had sin: but now they have no cloak for their sin. He that hateth me, hateth my Father also. If I had not done among them the works which none other man did, they had not had sin: but now have they both seen and hated both me and my Father. But this cometh to pass, that the word might be fulfilled that it is written in their law. They hated me without a cause. But when the Comforter is come, whom I will send unto you from the Father, even the spirit of truth, which proceedeth from the Father, he shall testify of me: and ye also shall bear witness, because ye have been with me from the beginning. These things have I spoken unto you, that ye should not be offended. They shall put you out of the synagogues: yea, the time cometh, that whosoever killeth you will think that he doeth God's service. And these things will they do unto you, because they have not known the Father nor me. But these things have I told you, that when the time shall come, ye may remember that

I told you of them. And these things I said not unto you at the beginning, because I was with you. But now I go my way to him that sent me; and none of you asketh me, Whither goest thou? But because I have said these things unto you, sorrow hath filled your heart. Nevertheless I tell you the truth; it is expedient for you that I go away: for if I go not away, the Comforter will not come unto you; but if I depart, I will send him unto you. And when he is come, he will reprove the world of sin, and of righteousness, and of judgment. Of sin, because they believe not on me; of righteousness, because I go to my Father, and ye see me no more; of judgment, because the prince of this world is judged. I have yet many things to say unto you, but ye cannot bear them now. Howbeit when he, the spirit of truth, is come, he will guide you into all truth: for he shall not speak of himself; but whatsoever he shall hear, that shall he speak: and he will shew you things to come. He shall glorify me; for he shall receive of mine, and shall shew it unto you. All things that the Father hath are mine; therefore said I, that he shall take of mine, and shall shew it unto you. A little while, and ye shall not see me; and again a little while, and ye shall see me, because I go to the Father. Then said some of his disciples among themselves, What is this that he saith unto us? A little while, and ye shall not see me; and again, a little while, and ye shall see me : and, Because I go to the Father ? They said therefore, What is this that he saith, A little while ? We cannot tell what he saith. Now Jesus knew that they were desirous to ask him, and said unto them ; Do ye enquire among yourselves of what I said, A little while, and ye shall not see me ; and again a little while, and ye shall see me ? Verily, verily, I say unto you, that ye shall weep and lament, but the world shall rejoice : and ye shall be sorrowful, but your sorrow shall be turned into joy. A woman when she is in travail hath sorrow, because her hour is come : but as soon as she is delivered of the child, she remembereth no more the anguish, for joy that a man is born into the world. And ye now therefore have sorrow : but I will see you again, and your heart shall rejoice, and your joy no man taketh from you. And in that day ye shall ask me nothing. Verily, verily, I say unto you, whatsoever ye shall ask the Father in my name, he will give it you. Hitherto have ye asked nothing in my name ; ask, and ye shall receive, that your joy may be full. These things I have spoken unto in proverbs : but the time cometh when I shall no more speak unto you in proverbs, but I shall shew you plainly of the Father. At that day ye shall ask in my name : and I say not unto you, that I will pray the Father for you : for the Father himself loveth you, because ye have loved me, and have believed that I came out from God. I came forth from the Father, and am come into the world: again, I leave the world, and go to the Father. His disciples said unto him, Lo, now speakest thou plainly, and speakest no proverb. Now are we sure that thou knowest all things, and needest not that any man should this: by this we believe that thou camest forth from God. Jesus answered them, Do ye now believe? Behold, the hour cometh, yea, is now come, that ye shall be scattered, every man to his own, and shall leave me alone: and yet I am not alone, because the Father is with me. These things I have spoken unto you, that in me ye might have peace. In the world ye shall have tribulation: but be of good cheer; I have overcome the world. These words spake Jesus, and lifted up his eyes to heaven, and said, Father, the hour is come; glorify thy Son, that thy Son may glorify thee; as thou hast given him power over all flesh, that he should give eternal life to as many as thou hast given him. And this is life eternal, that they might know thee, the only true God, and Jesus Christ, whom thou hast sent. I have glorified thee on the earth; I have finished the work which thou gavest me to do. And now O Father, glorify thou me with thine own self with the glory which I had with thee before the world was. I have manifested thy name unto the men which thou gavest me out of the world: thine they were, and thou gavest them me; and they have kept thy word. Now they have known that all things whatsoever thou hast given me are of thee.

For I have given unto them the words which thou gavest me; and they have received them, and have known surely that I came out from thee, and they have believed that thou didst sent me. I pray for them: I pray not for the world, but for them which thou hast given me! for they are thine. And all mine are thine, and thine are mine, and I am glorified in them. And now I am no more in the world, but these are in the world, and I come to thee. Holy Father, keep through thine own name those whom thou hast given me, that they may be one, as we are. While I was with them in the world, I kept them in thy name: those that thou gavest me I have kept, and none of them is lost, but the son of perdition! that the scripture might be fulfilled. And now came I to thee; and these things I speak in the world, that they might have my joy fulfilled in themselves. I have given them thy wolrd! and the word hath hated them, because they are not of the world, even as I am not of the world.

I pray not that thou shouldest take them out of the world, but that thou shouldest keep them from the evil. They are not of the world, even as I am not of the world. Sanctify them through thy truth: thy word is truth. As thou hast sent me into the world, even so have I also sent them into the world. And for them I sanctify myself, that they also might be sanctified through the truth.

Neither pray I for these alone, but for them also which shall believe on me through their word! that they all may be one! as thou, Father, art in me, and I in thee, that they also may be one in us: that the world may believe that thou hast sent me. And the glory which thou gavest me I have given them! that they may be one, even as we are one: I in them, and thou in me, that they may be made perfect in one: and that the world may know that thou hast sent me, and hast loved them, as thou hast loved me. Father, I will that they also, whom thou hast given me, be with me where I am! that they may behold my glory, which thou hast given me: for thou lovedst me before the foundation of the world. O righteous Father, the world hath not known thee: but I have known thee, and these have known that thou hast sent me. And I have declared unto them thy name, and I will declare it: that the love wherewith thou hast loved me may be in them, and I in them. When Jesus had spoken these words, he went forth with his disciples over the brook Cedron, where was a garden, into the which he entered, and his disciples.

Litany.

——o——

Psalm, xli, 1—13.

BLESSED is he that considereth the poor: the Lord will deliver him in time of trouble. The Lord

will preserve him, and keep him alive! and he shall be blessed upon the earth: and thou wilt not deliver him unto the will of his enemies. The Lord will strengthen him upon the bed of languishing: thou wilt make all his bed in his sickness. I said, Lord, be merciful unto me: heal my soul! for I have sinned against thee. Mine enemies speak evil of me: when shall he die, and his name perish! And if he come to see me, he speaketh vanity: his heart gathereth in iniquity to itself! When he goeth abroad, he telleth it. All that hate me whisper together against me: against me do they devise my hurt. And evil disease, say they, claveth fast unto him: and not that he lieth he shall rise up no more. Yea, mine own familiar friend, in whom I trusted, which did eat of my bread, lifted up his heel against me. But thou, O Lord, be merciful unto me, and raise me up, that I may requite them.
By this I know that thou favorest me, because mine enemy doth not triumph over me. And as for me, thou upholdest me in mine integrity, and settest me before thy face for ever. Blessed be the Lord God of Israel from everlasting, and to everlasting. Amen and Amen.

Psalm, xlii, 1—11.

AS the hart panteth after the waterbrooks, so panteth my soul after thee, O God. My soul thirsteth for God, for the living God: when shall I come and appear before God? My tears have been my meat day and night, while they continually say unto me, Where is the God? When I remember these things, I pour out my soul in me: for I had gone with the multitude. I went with them to the house of God, with the voice of joy and praise, with a multitude that kept holy day. Why are thou cast down, O my soul? and art thou disquieted in me? hope thou in God: for I shall yet praise him for the help of his countenance. O my God, my soul is cast down within me; therefore when I remember thee from the land of Jordan, and of the Hermonites from the land Mizah. Deep calleth unto deep at the noise of thy waterspouts: all thy waves and thy billows are gone over me. Yet the Lord will commend his loving kindness in the day time, and in the night his song shall be with me, and my prayer unto the God of my life. I will say unto God my rock, Why hast thou forgotten me? Why go I mourning because of the operation of the enemy? As with a sword in my bones, my enemies reproach me! while they say daily unto me, Where is thy God? Why art thou cast down, O my soul? and why art thou disquieted within me? hope thou in God: for I shall yet praise him, who is the health of my countenance, and my God.

Psalm, xliii, 1—5.

JUDGE me, O God, and plead my cause against an ungodly nation : O deliver me from the deceitful and unjust man. For thou art the God of my strength : why dost thou cast me of ? why go I mourning because of the operation of the enemy ? O send out thy light and truth : let them lead me ! let them bring me unto thy holy hill, and to thy tabernacles. They will I go into the altar of God, unto God my exceeding joy : yea, upon the harp will I praise thee, O God my God. Why art thou cast down, O my soul ? and why art thou disquieted within me ? hope in God : for I shall yet praise him, who is the help of my countenance, and my God.

—o—

Anthem.

AN evil disease, say they, cleaveth fast unto him. O Lord, O Lord, do not forsake me *(repeated thrice.)*—*Psalm, xli. 8.*

—o—

(Hymn of St. Nierses, continued from page 74).

VII.

HE fulfilled the Laws that were delivered to Moses at Sinai ; He ate the typical lamb and the unleavened bread with bitter herbs ; changing the old into new rites ; converting the shadow into light, and offering Himself instead of the lamb of the passover, as the Lamb of God.

VIII.

Instead of the unleavened bread He gave His own Divine Body—Virgin-born, immaculate, incorruptible. Instead of the blood of the sheep of the covenant, He offered His own Blood, as a new testament; instead of the bitterest endive He bequeathed as a substitute a pure and holy life.

IX.

The King of the Creation gave the Bread of Life to those who were hungry, and the Cup of Bliss to those who were afflicted as the children of Adam. "This is," said He, "the new covenant of My Blood, instead of the old covenant of blood, which ye shall keep in remembrance of Me, until I return among you again."

X.

We, who have assembled together, beseech Thee, together with the congregated eleven, on whom Thou hast bestowed Thy redeeming body with the cup; grant to us also, Oh Lord! with them the liberty of partaking at Thy table of the Bread of Life, which we desire, and the drink we thirst for.

XI.

From the chosen disciples, the holy Lambs, Judas separated himself, and the Lamb of God, the Bearer of our sins, was betrayed unto death for silver. To the Divine Supper the audacious and the proud traitor approached, and by dining with his Master he increased his perfidy.

XII.

The Light besought in a supplicating tone that the bewildered may be restored: "One of you, O Brethren!"

said He, " shall betray Me unto death." And Peter was alarmed; and beckoning John, asked him to question, who was to betray their Master.

St. Luke, xxii, 1—65.

NOW the feast of unleavened bread drew nigh, which is called the Passover. And the chief priests and scribes sought how they might kill him; for they feared the people. Then entered Satan into Judas surnamed Iscariot, being of the number of the twelve. And he went his way, and communed with the chief priests and captains how he might betray him unto them. And they were glad, and covenanted to give him money. And he promised, and sought opportunity to betray him unto them in the absence of the multitude. Then came the day of unleavened bread, when passover must be killed. And he sent Peter and John, saying, Go, and prepare us the passover, that we may eat. And they said unto him, Where wilt thou that we prepare? And he said unto them, Behold, when ye are entered into the city, there shall a man meet you, bearing a pitcher of water; follow him into the house where he entereth in. And ye shall say unto the good man of the house, The Master saith unto thee, Where is the guest chamber, where I shall eat the passover with my disciples? And he shall shew you a large upper room furnished: there make ready. And they went, and found as he had said unto them: and they made ready the passover. And when the hour was come, he sat down, and the twelve apostles with him. And he said unto them, With desire I have desired to eat this passover with you before I suffer: for I say unto you, I will not any more eat thereof, until it be fulfilled in the Kingdom of God. And he took the cup, and gave thanks, and said, Take this, and divide it among yourselves: for I say unto you, I will not drink of the fruit of the vine, until the Kingdom of God shall come. And he took bread, and gave thanks, and brake it, and gave unto them, saying this is my body which is given for you, this do in remembrance of me. Likewise also the cup after supper, saying this cup is the new testament in my blood, which is shed for you. But, behold, the hand of him that betrayeth me is with me on the table. And truly the Son of man goeth, as it was determined: but woe unto that man by whom he is betrayed. And they began to enquire among themselves which of them it was that should do this thing. And there was also a strife among them which of them should be accounted the greatest. And he said unto them, The Kings of the Gentiles exercise lordship over them; and they that excercise authority upon them are called benefactors. But ye shall not be so: but he that is greatest among you, let him be as the younger; and he that is chief, as he that doth serve. For whether is greater, he that sitteth at meat, or he that serveth? Is not he that sitteth at meat? but I am among you as he that serveth. Ye are they which have continued with me in my temptations. And I appoint unto you a kingdom, as my Father hath appointed unto me, that ye may eat and drink at my table in my Kingdom, and sit on thrones, judging the twelve tribes of Israel. And the Lord said, Simon, Simon, behold, Satan hath desired to have you, that he may sift you as wheat. But I have prayed for thee, that thy faith fail not: and when thou art converted strengthen they brethren. And he said unto him, Lord, I am ready to go with thee, both into prison, and to death. And he said, I tell thee, Peter, the cock shall not crow this day before that thou shalt thrice deny that thou knowest me. And he said unto them, When I sent you without purse, and scrip, and shoes, lacked ye anything? And they said, Nothing. Then said he unto them, But now, he that hath a purse, let him take it, and likewise his scrip: and he that hath no sword, let him sell his garment, and buy one. For I say unto you, that this that is written must yet be accomplished in me. And he was reckoned among the transgressors: for the things concerning me have an end. And they said, Lord, behold, here are two swords; and he said unto them, It is enough. And he came out, and went, as he was wont, to the Mount of Olives; and his disciples also followed him. And when he was at the place, he said unto them, Pray that ye enter not into temptation. And he was withdrawn from them about a stone's cast, and kneeled down, and prayed, saying, Father, if thou be willing, remove this cup from me: nevertheless not my will, but thine be done. And there appeared an angel unto him from heaven, strengthening him. And being in an agony he prayed more earnestly, and his sweat was as it were great drops of blood falling down to the ground. And when he rose up from prayer, and was come to his disciples, he found them sleeping for sorrow, and said unto them, Why sleep ye? rise and pray, lest ye enter into temptation. And while he yet spake, behold a multitude, and he that was called Judas, one of the twelve, went before them, and drew near unto Jesus to kiss him. But Jesus said unto him, Judas, betrayest thou the Son of man with a kiss? When they which were about him saw what would follow, they said unto him, Lord, shall we smite with the sword? And one of them smote the servant of the high priest, and cut off his right ear. And Jesus answered and said, Suffer ye thus far. And he touched his ear, and healed him. Then Jesus said unto the chief priests, and captains of the temple, and the elders, which were come to him, Be ye come out, as against a thief, with swords and staves? When I was daily with you in the temple, ye stretched forth no hands against me: but this is your hour, and the power of darkness. Then took they him, and led him, and brought him into the high priest's house; and

Peter followed afar off. And when they had kindled a fire in the midst of the hall, and were sat down together, Peter sat down among them. But a certain maid beheld him as he sat by the fire, and earnestly looked upon him, and said, This man was also with him. And he denied him, saying, Woman, I know him not. And after a little while another saw him, and said, Thou art also of them. And Peter said, Man, I am not. And about the space of an hour after another confidently affirmed, saying, Of a truth this fellow also was with him: for he is a Galilean. And Peter said, Man, I know not what thou sayest. And immediately, while he yet spake, the cock crew. And the Lord turned, and looked upon Peter. And Peter remembered the words of the Lord, how he had said unto him, Before the cock crow, thou shalt deny me thrice. And Peter went out, and wept bitterly. And the men that held Jesus mocked him, and smote him. And when they had blindfolded him, they struck him on the face, and asked him, saying, Prophesy who is that smote thee? And many other things blasphemously spake they against him.

Litany.

——o——

Psalm, lix, 1—17.

DELIVER me from mine enemies, O my God: defend me from them that rise up against me. Deliver me from the workers of iniquity, and save me from bloody men. For, lo, they lie in wait for my soul: the mighty are gathered against me; not for my transgression, nor for my sin, O Lord. They run and prepare themselves without my fault; awake to help me, and behold. Thou therefore, O Lord God of hosts, the God of Israel, awake to visit all the heathen: be not merciful to any wicked transgressors. They return at evening: they make a noise like a dog, and go round about the city. Behold, they belch out with their mouth: swords are in their lips: for who, say they, doth hear? But thou, O Lord, shalt laugh at them: thou shalt have all the heathen in derision. Because of his strength will I wait upon thee: for God is my defence. The God of my mercy shall prevent me: God shall let me see my desire upon mine enemies. Slay them not, lest my people forget: scatter them by thy power; and bring them down, O Lord our shield. For the sin of their mouth and the words of their lips let them even be taken in their pride: and for cursing and lying which they speak. Consume them in wrath, consume them, that they may not be: and let them know that God ruleth in Jacob unto the ends of the earth. And at evening let them return; and let them make a noise like a dog, and go round about the city. Let them wander up and down for meat, and grudge if they be not satisfied. But I will sing of thy power; yea, I will sing aloud of thy mercy in the morning: for thou hast been my defence and refuge in the day of my trouble. Unto thee, O my strength, will I sing: for God is my defence, and the God of my mercy.

Psalm, lx, 1—12.

O GOD thou hast cast us off, thou hast scattered us, thou hast been displeased; O turn thyself to us again. Thou hast made the earth to tremble; thou hast broken it: heal the breaches thereof; for it shaketh. Thou hast shewed thy people hard things: thou hast made us to drink the wine of astonishment. Thou hast given a banner to them that fear thee, that it may be displayed because of the truth, that thy beloved may be delivered; save with thy right hand, and hear me. God hath spoken in his holiness; I will rejoice, I will divide Shechem, and mete out the valley of Succoth. Gilead is mine, and Manasseh is mine; Ephraim also is the strength of mine head; Judah is my lawgiver; Moab is my washpot; over Edom will I cast-out my shoe; Philistia, triumph thou because of me. Who will bring me into the strong city? Who will lead me into Edom? Wilt not thou, O God, which hadst cast us off? and thou, O God, which didst not go out with our armies? Give us help from trouble: for vain is the help of man. Through God we shall do valiantly: for he it is that shall tread down our enemies.

———o———

Psalm lxi, 1—8.

HEAR my cry, O God; attend unto my prayer. From the end of the earth will I cry unto thee when my heart is overwhelmed: lead me to the rock that is higher than I. For thou hast been a shelter for me, and a strong tower from the enemy. I will abide in thy tabernacle for ever: I will trust in the covert of thy wings. For thou, O God, hast heard my vows: thou hast given me the heritage of those that fear thy name. Thou wilt prolong the king's life: and his years as many generations. He shall abide before God for ever. O prepare mercy and truth, which may preserve him. So will I sing praise unto thy name for ever, that I may daily perform my vows.

―――o―――

Anthem.

DELIVER me from mine enemies, O my God: defend me from them that rise up against me (*repeated thrice*).—*Psalm, lxiii, 1.*

―――o―――

(*Hymn of St. Nierses continued from page 90.*)

XIII.

WITH an affectionate care for his favourite disciples, Christ dispelled their anxiety by giving a piece of soaked bread to Judas, as a sign to distinguish the secret traitor, who on receiving the sop was stript of the Grace of the Divine Spirit, and delivered himself over to the devil by betraying his Master.

XIV.

When deprived of the Supreme Light the Lover of Darkness went out. The Lord warned his enlightened disciples against their being offended because of Him that night. Peter repudiated the thought rashly, but was afterwards reproached by the crowing of the cock. Then Christ spake of His own departure from this world, and of the coming of the Holy Ghost.

XV.

Christ went from the mystic Upper-room to the other side of the vale of Cedron, and entering the garden, instead of the garden of Eden, he replaced Adam in it. Introduce us there with him O Lord! that we may enjoy once more the inheritance of our paternal mansion.

XVI.

Our Lord began to be serious and thoughtful of His passions; he withdrew apart with only three of His disciples. "To save the world, My soul is willing, but the flesh is weak." Not that the one was powerful and strong, and the other weak and vulnerable, but both unitedly and willingly bore the sufferings.

XVII.

He prayed for me in a tone of devotion to His Essential Father; He humbly knelt, though the veneration of the universe was due to Him. "If the salvation of mankind can be effected without any suffering, as it is written, let the cup of death pass away from Me, not My will, but Thy will be done."

XVIII.

Plunged in fear, our Lord was covered with perspiration, which trickled down and fell like pearls. But to strengthen Him an Angel came, that the prophetical books may be fulfilled. As the Word of God took the complete nature of man, so it was incumbent on Him to suffer fear and sorrow in His Incarnation.

St. Mark, xiv, 27—72.

AND Jesus saith unto them, All ye shall be offended because of me this night: for it is written, I will smite the shepherd, and the sheep shall be scattered. But after that I am risen, I will go before you into Galilee. But Peter said unto them, Although all shall be offended, yet will not I. And Jesus saith unto him, Verily I say unto thee, that this day, even in this night, before the cock crow twice, thou shalt deny me thrice. But he spake the more vehemently, if I should die with thee, I will not deny thee in any wise. Likewise also said they all. And they came to a place which was named Gethsemane: and he saith to his disciples, Sit ye here, while I shall pray. And he taketh with him Peter and James and John, and began to be sore amazed, and to be very heavy; and saith unto them, My soul is exceeding sorrowful unto death: tarry ye here, and watch. And he went forward a little, and fell on the ground, and prayed that, if it were possible, the hour might pass from him. And he said, Abba, Father, all things are possible unto thee; take away this cup from me: nevertheless not what I will, but what thou wilt. And he cometh, and findeth them sleeping, and saith unto Peter, Simon sleepest thou? Couldest not thou watch one hour? Watch ye and pray, lest ye enter into temptation. The spirit truly is ready, but the flesh is weak. And again he went away, and prayed, and spake the same words. And when he returned, he found them asleep again (for their eyes were heavy); neither wist they what to answer him. And he cometh the third time, and saith unto them, Sleep on now, and take your rest: it is enough, the hour is come; behold, the Son of man is betrayed into the hands of sinners. Rise up, let us go; lo, he that betrayeth me is at hand. And immediately, while he yet spake, cometh Judas, one of the twelve, and with him a great multitude with swords and staves, from the chief priests and the scribes and the elders. And he that betrayeth him had given them a token, saying, Whomsoever I shall kiss, that same is he, take him, and lead him away safely. And as soon as he was come, he goeth straightway to him, and saith, Master, master; and kissed him. And they laid their hands on him, and took him. And one of them that stood by drew a sword, and smote a servant of the high priest, and cut off his ear. And Jesus answered and said unto them, Are ye come out, as against a thief, with swords and with staves to take me? I was daily with you in the temple teaching, and ye tooks me not: but the scriptures must be fulfilled. And they all forsook him, and fled. And there followed him a certain young man, having a linen cloth cast about his naked body; and the young men laid hold upon him. And he left the linen cloth, and fled from them naked. And they led Jesus away to the high priest: and with him were assembled all the chief priests and the elders and the scribes. And Peter followed him afar off, even into the palace of the high priest: and he sat with the servants, and warmed himself at the fire. And the chief priests and all the council sought for witness against Jesus to put him to death; and found none; for many bore false witness against him, but their witness agreed not together. And there arose certain; and bore false witness against him, saying, We heard him say, I will destroy this temple that is made with hands, and within three days I will build another made without hands. But neither so did their witness agree together. And the high priest stood up in the midst, and asked Jesus, saying, Answerest thou nothing? What is it which these witness against thee? But he held his peace, and answered nothing. Again the high priest asked him, and said unto him, Art thou the Christ, the Son of the Blessed? And Jesus said, I am; and ye shall see the Son of man sitting on the right hand of power, and coming in the clouds of heaven. Then the high priest rent his clothes, and saith, What need we any further witness? Ye have heard the blasphemy: what think ye? And they all condemned him to be guilty of death. And some began to spit on him, and to cover his face, and to buffet him, and to say unto him, Prophesy: and the servants did strike him with the palms of their hands. And as Peter was beneath in the palace, there cometh one of the maids of the high priest. And when she saw Peter warming himself she looked upon him, and said, And thou also was with Jesus of Nazareth. But he denied, saying, I know not, neither understand I what thou sayest. And he went out into the porch; and the cock crew. And a maid saw him again, and began to say to them that stood by, This is one of them. And he denied it again. And a little after, they that stood by said again to Peter, Surely thou art one of them; for thou art a Galilian, and thy speech agreeth thereto. But he began to curse and to swear, saying, I know not this man of whom ye speak. And the second time the cock crew. And Peter called to mind the words that Jesus said unto him, Before the cock crow twice, thou shalt deny me thrice. And when he thought thereon, he wept.

Litany.

— o —

Psalm, lxxix, 1—13.

O GOD, the heathen are come into thine inheritance; thy holy temple have they defiled; they have laid Jerusalem on heaps. The dead bodies of thy servants have they given to be meat unto the fowls of the heaven, the flesh of thy saints unto the beasts of the earth. Their blood have they shed like water round about Jerusalem; and there was none to bury them. We are become a reproach to our neighbours, a scorn and derision to them that are round about us. How long, Lord, wilt thou be angry for ever? Shall thy jealousy burn like fire? Pour out thy wrath upon the heathen that have not known thee, and upon the kingdoms that have not called upon thy name. For they have devoured Jacob, and laid waste his dwelling place. O remember not against us former iniquities: let thy tender mercies speedily prevent us: for we are brought very low. Help us, O God of our salvation, for the glory of thy name, and deliver us, and purge away our sins, for thy name's sake. Wherefore should the heathen say. Where is their God? Let him be known among the heathen in our sight by the revenging of the blood of thy servants which is shed. Let the sighing of the prisoner come before thee; according to the greatness of thy power preserve thou those that are appointed to die; and render unto our neighbours sevenfold into their bosom their reproach, wherewith they have reproached thee, O Lord. Lo! we thy people and sheep of thy pasture will give thee thanks for ever: we will shew forth thy praise to all generations.

Psalm, lxxx, 1—19.

GIVE ear, O shepherd of Israel, thou that leadest Joseph like a flock; thou that dwellest between the cherubims, shine forth. Before Ephraim and Benjamin and Manasseh stir up thy strength, and come and save us. Turn us again, O God, and cause thy face to shine; and we shall be saved. Lord God of hosts, how long wilt thou be angry against the prayer of thy people? Thou feedest them with the bread of tears; and givest them tears to drink in great measure. Thou makest us a strife unto our neighbours: and our enemies laugh among themselves. Turn us again, O God of hosts, and cause thy face to shine; and we shall be saved. Thou hast brought a vine out of Egypt: thou hast cast out the heathen, and planted it. Thou preparedst room before it, and didst cause it to take deep root, and it filled the land. The hills were covered with the shadow of it, and the boughs thereof were like the goodly cedars. She sent out her boughs unto the sea, and her branches unto the river. Why hast thou then broken down her hedges, so that all they which pass by the way do pluck her? The boar out of the wood doth waste it, and the wild beast of the field doth devour it. Return, we beseech thee, O God of hosts, look down from heaven, and behold, and visit this vine; and the vineyard which thy right hand hath planted, and the branch that thou madest strong for thyself. It is burned with fire; it is cut down; they perish at the rebuke of thy countenance. Let thy hand be upon the man of thy right hand, upon the Son of man whom thou madest strong for thyself. So will not we go back from thee: quicken us, and we will call upon thy name. Turn us again, O Lord God of hosts; cause thy face to shine; and we shall be saved.

Psalm, lxxxi, 1—16.

SING aloud unto God our strength: make a joyful noise unto the God of Jacob. Take a psalm, and bring hither the timbrel, the pleasant harp with the psaltery. Blow up the trumpet in the new moon, in the time appointed, on our solemn feast day. For this was a statute for Israel, and a law of the God of Jacob. This he ordained in Joseph for a testimony when he went out through the land of Egypt: where I heard a language that I understood not. I removed his shoulder from the burden; his hands were delivered from the pots. Thou calledst in trouble, and I delivered thee; I answered thee in the secret place of thunder: I proved thee at the waters of Meribah. Hear, O my people, and I will testify unto thee: O Israel, if thou wilt hearken unto me, there shall no strange God be in thee; neither shalt thou worship any strange god. I am the Lord thy God, which brought thee out of the land of Egypt: open thy mouth wide, and I will fill it. But my people would not hearken to my voice; and Israel would none of me. So I gave them up unto their own hearts' lust: and they walked in their own counsels. O that my people had hearkened unto me, and Israel had walked in my ways! I should soon have subdued their enemies, and turned my hand against their adversaries. The haters of the Lord should have submitted themselves unto him: but their time should have endureth for ever. He should have fed them also with the finest of the wheat: and with honey out of the rock should I have satisfied thee.

—o—

Anthem.

THEY were rejected from thy hand, we are thy people and sheep of thy pasture *(repeated thrice).*—Psalm, lxxix, 13.

—o—

(Hymn of St. Nierses continued from page 99).

XIX.

O Thou, the ray of God's glory! who in the nature of man was tormented in that night, and who prayed to the Heavenly Father, penetrate us with Thy heavenly light;

destroy the fear of the wicked, and bind every part of my body and soul with the righteous fear of Thee.

XX.

Judas, who was to betray Christ, approached with a band of Pharisees, and fell like the fallen angels, never to rise again. Judas perfidiously kissed Our Lord as a signal that the opportunity of compassing Christ's death was at hand.

Instead of loving, he betrayed his Master, returning ill or good.

XXI.

Then Peter, with a loving tenderness for Christ, cut off with his sword the right ear of the servant, Malchus, that ear which did not hear the Lord. Our Lord, soon approaching, touched the ear as a physician, and cured as a god; which beneficence his blind assailants could not see.

XXII.

When the small New Flock was scattered because the Good Shepherd was smitten, Peter alone followed Christ, and the rock was shakened by a mere girl. When the predicted cock crew, Our Lord looked at Peter, who, recollecting the words of Christ, wept bitterly and recovered from falling.

XXIII.

O Thou! who hast forgiven the rock of the Church, sustained him from falling, and made him stand from slipping down, because he heartily wept in repentance; raise me also, O Lord! like him, from the fall occasioned by him who first caused man to stumble; give abundance of tears to my eyes, and pour on my head the water of the ocean.

XXIV.

O Thou! who voluntarily gavest thy unfastenable Hands to be tied, those Hands which could release all bands; who was taken to the palace of Caiphas and Annanias; whom the servant struck on the face, that Face from which the Seraphim sheltered their faces with their wings; spitting upon that Face with impure mouth, which by spit recovered the sight of the blind.

St. Matthew, xxvi, 31—56.

THEN saith Jesus unto them, All ye shall be offended because of me this night: for it is written, I will smite the shepherd, and the sheep of the flock shall be scattered abroad. But after I am risen again, I will go before you into Galilee. Peter answered and said unto him, Though all men shall be offended because of thee yet will I never be offended. Jesus said unto him, Verily I say unto thee, that this night, before the cock crow, thou shalt deny me thrice. Peter said unto him, Though I should die with thee, yet will I not deny thee. Likewise also said all the disciples. Then cometh Jesus with them unto a place called Gethsemane, and saith unto the disciples, Sit ye here, while I go and pray yonder. And he took with him Peter and the two sons of Zebedee, and began to be sorrowful and very heavy. Then saith he unto them, My soul is exceeding sorrowful, even unto death : tarry ye here, and watch with me. And he went a little farther, and fell on his face, and prayed, saying, O my Father, if it be possible, let this cup pass from me : nevertheless not as I will but as thou wilt. And he cometh unto the disciples and findeth them asleep, and saith unto Peter, What could ye not watch with me one hour? Watch and pray, that ye enter not into temptation : the spirit indeed is willing, but the flesh is weak. He went away again the second time, and prayed, saying, O my Father, if this cup may not pass away from me, except I drink it, thy will be done. And he came and found them asleep again : for their eyes were heavy. And he left them, and went away again, and prayed the third time, saying the same words. Then cometh he to his disciples, and saith unto them, Sleep on now, and take your rest : behold, the hour is at hand, and the Son of man is betrayed into the hands of sinners. Rise, let us be going : behold, he is at hand that doth betray me. And while he yet spake, lo ! Judas, one of the twelve, came, and with him a great multitude with swords and staves, from the chief priests and elders of the people. Now he that betrayed him gave them a sign, saying, whomsoever I shall kiss, that same is he : hold him fast. And forthwith he came to Jesus, and said, Hail, Master, and kissed him. And Jesus said unto him, Friend, wherefore art thou come? Then came they, and laid hands on Jesus and took him. And, behold, one of them which were with Jesus stretched out his hand, and drew his sword, and struck a servant of the high priest's, and smote off his ear. Then said Jesus unto him, Put up again thy sword into his place: for all they that take the sword shall perish with the sword. Thinkest thou that I cannot now pray to my Father, and he shall presently give me more than twelve legions of angels? But how then shall the scriptures be fulfilled, that thus it must be? In that same hour said Jesus to the multitude, Are ye come out as against a thief with swords and staves for to take me? I sat daily with you teaching in the temple, and ye laid no hold on me. But all this was done, that the scriptures of the prophets might be fulfilled. Then all the disciples forsook him, and fled.

Litany.

———o———

Psalm, cix, 1—31.

HOLD not thy peace, O God of my praise; for the mouth of the wicked and the mouth of the deceitful are opened against me: they have spoken against me with a lying tongue. They compassed me about also with words of hatred; and fought against me without a cause. For my love they are my adversaries: but I give myself unto prayer. And they have rewarded me evil for good, and hatred for my love. Set thou a wicked man over him: and let Satan stand at his right hand. When he shall be judged, let him be condemned: and let his prayer become sin. Let his days be few; and let another take his office. Let his children be fatherless, and his wife a widow. Let his children be continually vagabonds, and beg: let them seek their bread also out of their desolate places. Let the extortioner catch all that he hath; and let the strangers spoil his labour. Let there be none to extend mercy unto him: neither let there be any to favour his fatherless children. Let his posterity be cut off; and in the generation following let their name be blotted out. Let the iniquity of his fathers be remembered with the Lord; and let not the sin of his mother be blotted out. Let them be before the Lord continually, that he may cut off the memory of them from the earth, because that he remembered not to shew mercy, but persecuted the poor and needy man, that he might even slay the broken in heart. As he loved cursing, so let it come unto him: as he delighted not in blessing, so let it be far from him. As he clothed himself with cursing like as with his garment, so let it come into his bowels like water, and like oil into his bones. Let it be unto him as the garment which covereth him, and for a girdle wherewith he is girded continually. Let this be the reward of mine adversaries from the Lord, and of them that speak evil against my soul. But do thou for me,

O God the Lord, for thy name's sake: because thy mercy is good, deliver thou me. For I am poor and needy, and my heart is wounded within me. I am gone like the shadow when it declineth: I am tossed up and down as the locust. My knees are weak through fasting; and my flesh faileth of fatness. I became also a reproach unto them: when they looked upon me they shaked their heads. Help me, O Lord my God: O save me according to thy mercy, that they may know that this is thy hand; that thou, Lord, hast done it. Let them curse, but bless thou: when they arise, let them be ashamed; but let thy servant rejoice. Let mine adversaries be clothed with shame, and let them cover themselves with their own confusion, as with a mantle. I will greatly praise the Lord with my mouth; yea, I will praise him among the multitude. For he shall stand at the right hand of the poor, to save him from those that condemn his soul.

Psalm, cx, 1—7.

THE Lord said unto my Lord, Sit thou at my right hand, until I make thine enemies thy footstool. The Lord shall send the rod of thy strength out of Zion: rule thou in the midst of thine enemies. Thy people shall be willing in the day of thy power, in the beauties of holiness from the womb of the morning: thou hast the dew of thy youth. The Lord hath sworn, and will not repent, Thou art a priest for ever after the order of Melchizedek. The Lord at thy right hand shall strike through kings in the day of his wrath. He shall judge among the heathen; he shall fill the places with the dead bodies; he shall wound the heads over many countries; he shall drink of the brook in the way: therefore shall he lift up the head.

Psalm, cxi, 1—10.

PRAISE ye the Lord, I will praise the Lord with my whole heart, in the assembly of the upright, and in the congregation. The works of the Lord are great, sought out of all them that have pleasure therein. His work is honourable and glorious: and his righteousness endureth for ever. He hath made his wonderful works to be remembered: the Lord is gracious and full of compassion. He hath given meat unto them that fear him: he will ever be mindful of his covenant. He hath shewed his people the power of his works, that he may give them the heritage of the heathen. The works of his hands are verity and judgment; all his commandments are sure. They stand fast for ever and ever, and are done in truth and uprightness. He sent redemption unto his people: he hath commanded his covenant for ever: holy and reverend is his name. The fear of the Lord is the beginning of wisdom: a good understanding have all they that do his commandments: his praise endureth for ever.

Anthem.

THEY have spoken against me with a lying tongue. They compassed me about also with words of hatred (*repeated thrice*).—*Psalm, cix, 2—3.*

Hymn of St. Nierses, (continued from page 108.)

XXV.

O THOU! the Releaser of man from Evil Bondage! who was bound instead of the bound Adam, absolve me from the chain of hellish sins which I have willingly tied round me; Thou, who for the debt of the sin of Adam, stoodst, though innocent, before the tribunal of the High Priest, when Thou comest again in Thy paternal glory, do not judge me with sinners.

XXVI.

O Thou! who was ridiculed for the sins of old Adam, blot out from my face the shameful sins committed through impudence; Thou, who hast forgiven the wicked servant the blow on Thy face, strike forcibly the wicked devil, as He forcibly struck my face.

XXVII.

The Crest of Light on the morning of the Friday of the ancient Easter, stood before the judge, the servant sitting in judgment; and, when questioned by Pilate, He returned no answer, that what was written might be fulfilled. "He was like unto a man that spake not."

XXVIII.

The rabble of soldiery dressed Him in a garment of

reproach, Him whose dress was rays of light cast like a mantle over the body. The rabble knelt in mockery, and struck Him with a reed on His Head and crowned with a crown of thorns Him who was to remove the thorns of our sins.

XXIX.

The terror of the Cherubim willingly bore the wooden cross to the place of Golgotha, where the first man was laid. They gave Him to drink wine mixed with myrrh and food with gall ; by which the bitterness of the forbidden fruit was changed into an agreeable and sweet savor.

XXX.

The Celestials were frightened when they saw our Lord naked, and his dress distributed, and lots cast on his garments. His Feet and Hands were pierced according to the inspired carols of David ; and those fingers were nailed on the cross which wrote the Commandments on the Tables.

St. Matthew, xxvi, 57—75.

AND they that had laid hold on Jesus led him away to Caiaphas, the high priest, where the scribes and elders were assembled. But Peter followed him afar off unto the high priest's palace, and went in, and sat with the servants, to see the end. Now the chief priests, and elders, and all the counsel, sought false witness against Jesus, to put him to death. But found none : yea, though many false witnesses came, yet found they none. At the last came two false witnesses ; and said, This fellow said, I am able to destroy the temple of God, and to build it in three days. And the high priest arose, and said unto him, Answerest thou nothing? What is it which these witness against thee? But Jesus held his peace. And the high priest answered and said unto him, I adjure thee, by the living God, that thou tell us whether thou be the Christ, the Son of God. Jesus said unto him, Thou hast said: nevertheless I say unto you, hereafter shall ye see the Son of man sitting on the right hand of power, and coming in the clouds of heaven. Then the high priest rent his clothes, saying, He hath spoken blasphemy. What further need have we of witnesses? Wehold, now ye have heard his blasphemy. What think ye? They answered and said, He is guilty of death. Then did they spit in his face, and buffeted him! and others smote him with the palms of their hand, saying, Prophesy unto us, thou Christ, who is he that smote thee? Now Peter sat without in the palace, and a damsel came unto him, saying, Thou also was with Jesus of Galilee. But he denied before them all, saying, I know not what thou sayest. And when he was gone out into the porch, another maid saw him, and said unto them that were there, This fellow was also with Jesus of Nazareth. And again he denied with an oath, I do not know the man. And after a while came unto him they that stood by, and said to Peter, Surely thou also art one of them! For

HOLY THURSDAY NIGHT. 117

thy speech betrayeth thee. Then he began to curse and to swear, saying, I know not the man. And immediately the cock crew. And Peter remembered the words of Jesus which saith unto him, Before the cock crows, thou shalt deny me thrice. And he went out, and wept bitterly.

Litany.

———o———

Psalm, cxviii, 1—19.

O GIVE thanks unto the Lord; for he is good: because his mercy endureth for ever. Let Israel now say, that his mercy endureth for ever. Let the house of Aaron now say, that his mercy endureth for ever. Let them now that fear the Lord say, that his mercy endureth for ever. I called upon the Lord in distress: the Lord answered me, and set in a large place. The Lord is on my side; I will not fear: what can man do unto me? The Lord taketh my part with them that help me: therefore shall I see my desire upon them that hate me. It is better to trust in the Lord than to put confidence in man. It is better to trust in the Lord than to put confidence in princes. All nations compassed me about; but in the name of the Lord will I destroy them. They compassed me about; yea, they compassed me about: but in the name of the Lord I will destroy them. They compassed me about like bees; they are quenched as the fire of thorns: for in the name of the

Lord I will destroy them. Thou hast thrust sore at me that I might fall: but the Lord helped me. The Lord is my strength and song, and is become my salvation. The voice of rejoicing and salvation is in the tabernacles of the righteous: the right hand of the Lord doeth valiantly. I shall not die, but live, and declare the works of the Lord. The Lord hath chastened me sore: but he hath not given me over unto death. Open to me the gates of righteousness: I will go into them, and I will praise the Lord.

Anthem.

O GIVE thanks unto the Lord; for he is good: because his mercy endureth for ever (*repeated thrice*).—*Psalm, cxviii, 1—23.*

Hymn of St. Nierses, (continued from page 115.)

XXXI.

HIS Hands were extended for the hands of Adam, His Feet for the feet of Adam that walked to the forbidden tree, the wood of the cross for the wood of the bitter fruit, and life exchanged for death. Between two criminals the Lawgiver stood naked, which mystery, none of the blind nation saw except one of the robbers.

XXXII.

The sun of our system turned the day into night, the veil of darkness covered Christ's nakedness, that the unworthy eye might not behold it. The sun was darkened in his meridian when Adam suffered death for his sin, and in the ninth hour it turned into light when death was overcome by death.

XXXIII.

The Mother of our Lord, who stood near the cross, shed tears of compassion when she heard her Only Begotten Son complain of thirst and they gave Him vinegar mixed with gall, Him who made rivers flow through Eden ; who gave to the maddened race a wholesome drink from the rock.

XXXIV.

At the third hour the serpent beguiled the mind of our old mother Eve. At the sixth hour the first man fell by her persuasive words, and at the same hour the Lord was crucified to atone for their sin ; and when old Adam came out of Eden, the robber was placed there.

XXXV.

Our Lord cried for me compassionately, exclaimed to His Father : " Eloi, Eloi," and willingly gave up His ghost to His Father, to whose hands He committed the souls of mankind. The Earth shook from its foundation, the veil was rent through, rocks burst asunder, and the graves of death opened.

XXXVI.

He was proclaimed by the miracles He wrought to be God crucified in body for me ; He died in our nature, though acknowledged to be Immortal God. By the two streams which flowed from His side, His Church is established; water for purification, and blood for drink, that the Son may be glorified with the Father.

---o---

St. John, xviii, 2--27.

AND Judas also, which betrayed him, knew the place: for Jesus ofttimes resorted thither with his disciples. Judas then, having received a band of men and officers from the chief priests and Pharisees, cometh thither with lanterns and torches and weapons. Jesus therefore, knowing all things that should come upon him, went forth, and said unto them, Whom seek ye? They answered him, Jesus of Nazareth. Jesus saith unto them, I am he. And Judas also, which betrayed him, stood with them. As soon then as he had said unto them I am he, they went backward, and fell to the ground. Then asked he them again, Whom seek ye? And they said, Jesus of Nazareth. Jesus answered, I have told you that I am he: if therefore ye seek me, let these go their way, that the saying might be fulfilled which he spake. Of them which thou gavest me have I lost none. Then Simon Peter having a sword drew it, and smote the high priest and cut off his right ear. The servant's name was Malchus. Then said Jesus unto Peter, Put up thy sword into the sheath: the cup which my Father hath given me, shall I not drink it?

Then the band and the captain and officers of the Jews took Jesus, and bound him, and led him away to Annas first; for he was father-in-law to Caiaphas, which was the high priest that same year. Now Caiaphas was he which gave counsel to the Jews that it was expedient that one man should die for the people. And Simon Peter followed Jesus, and so did another disciple: that disciple was known unto the high priest, and went in with Jesus into the palace of the high priest. But Peter stood at the door without. Then went out that other disciple, which was known unto the high priest, and spake unto her that kept the door, and brought in Peter. Then saith the damsel that kept the door unto Peter, Art not thou also one of this man's disciples? He saith, I am not. And the servants and officers stood there, who had made a fire of coals; for it was cold: and they warmed themselves: and Peter stood with them, and warmed himself. The high priest then asked Jesus of his disciples, and of his doctrine. Jesus answered him, I spake openly to the world; I ever taught in the synagogue, and in the temple, whither the Jews always resort; and in secret have I said nothing. Why askest thou me? Ask them which heard me what I have said unto them: behold, they know what I said. And when he had thus spoken, one of the officers which stood by struck Jesus with the palm of his hand, saying,

Answerest thou the high priest so? Jesus answered him, If I have spoken evil, bear witness of the evil: but if well, why smitest thou me? Now Annas had sent him bound unto Caiaphas, the high priest. And Simon Peter stood and warmed himself. They said therefore unto him, Art not thou also one of his discicples? He denied it and said, I am not. One of the servants of the high priest, being his kinsman, whose ear Peter cut off, said, Did not I see thee in the garden with him? Peter then denied again: and immediately the cock crew.

―o―

Supplication by the Priest.
Exhortation by the Deacon.
Prayer by the Priest.

―o―

Anthem.

PRINCES have persecuted me without a cause: but my heart standeth in awe of thy word. Alleluia. I rejoice at thy word, as one that findeth great spoil. Alleluia. I hate and abhor lying: but thy law do I love. Alleluia. Seven times a day do I praise thee because of thy righteous judgments. Alleluia. Great peace have they which love thy law: and nothing shall offend them. Alleluia. Lord, I have hoped for thy salvation, and done thy commandments. Alleluia. My soul hath kept thy testimonies; and I love them exceedingly. Alleluia. I have kept thy precepts and the testimonies : for all my ways are before thee. Alleluia.

LET my cry come near before thee, O Lord; give me understanding according to thy word. Alleluia, Alleluia. Let my supplication come before thee; deliver me according to thy word. Alleluia, Alleluia. My lips shall utter praise when thou hast taught me thy statutes. Alleluia, Alleluia. My tongue shall speak of thy word; for all thy commandments are righteousness. Alleluia, Alleluia. Let thine hand help me ; for I have chosen thy precepts. Alleluia, Alleluia. I have longed for thy salvation, O Lord; and thy law is my delight. Alleluia, Alleluia. Let my soul live, and it shall praise thee ; and let thy judgments help me. Alleluia, Alleluia. I have gone astray like a lost sheep ; seek thy servant; for I do not forget thy commandments. Alleluia, Alleluia.—*Psalm, cxix,* 161, 176.

Exhortation by the Deacon.
Prayer by the Priest.
Hymn of St. Isaac.
Supplication by the Priest.
Exhortation by the Deacon.
Prayer by the Priest.

Anthem.

Alleluia, Alleluia, Alleluia.

THOU didst ride upon thine horses and thy chariots of salvation. Thy brow was made quite naked, according to the oaths of the tribes, even thy word. Thou didst cleave the earth with rivers. The mountains saw thee, and they trembled: the overflowing of the water passed by: the deep uttered his voice, and lifted up his hands on high. The sun and moon stood still in their habitation.—*Habakkuk, iii, 8—11.*

Psalm, lxxxviii, 8—9.

Alleluia, Alleluia, Alleluia.

I AM shut up, and I cannot come forth; mine eye mourneth by reason of affliction. Lord, I have called daily upon thee; I have stretched out my hands unto thee. Glory, etc. Alleluia (*repeated thrice*).—*Psalm, lxxxviii, 8—9.*

—o—

Prayers by the Priest "Our Father."
The Song of the three Holy Children, Shadrach, Meshach and Abednego.

—o—

Daniel, iii, 52—88.

BLESSED art thou, O Lord God of our fathers: thy name is worthy to be praised and glorified for evermore: for thou art righteous in all the things that thou hast done to us; yea, true are all thy works, thy ways are right, and all thy judgment truth. In all the things that thou hast brought upon us and upon the holy city of our fathers, even Jerusalem, thou hast executed true judgment: for according to truth and judgment didst thou bring all these things upon us because of our sins. For we have sinned and committed iniquity, departing from thee. In all things have we trespassed, and not obeyed thy commandments, nor kept them, neither done as thou hast commanded us, that it might go well with us. Wherefore all that thou hast brought upon us, and everything that thou hast done to us, thou hast done in true judgment. And thou didst deliver us into the hands of lawless enemies, most hateful forsakers of God and to an unjust king, and the most wicked in all the world. And now we cannot open our mouths; we are become a shame and reproach to thy servants, and to them that worship thee. Yet deliver us not up wholly, for thy name's sake, neither disannul thou thy covenant: and cause not thy mercy to depart from us, for thy beloved Abraham's sake, for thy servant Isaac's sake, and for thy holy Israel's sake; to whom thou hast spoken and promised, that thou wouldst multiply their seed as the stars of heaven, and as the sand that lieth upon the sea shore. For we, O Lord, are become less than any nation, and be kept under this day in all the world because of our sins.

Neither is there at this time prince, or prophet, or leader, or burnt offering, or sacrifice, or oblation, or incense, or place to sacrifice before thee, and to find mercy. Nevertheless in a contrite heart and an humble spirit let us be accepted. Like as in the burnt offering of rams and bullocks, and like as in ten thousands of fat lambs, so let our sacrifice be in thy sight this day, and grant that we may wholly go after thee: for they shall not be confounded that put their trust in thee. And now we follow thee with all our hearts; we fear thee and seek thy face. Put us not to shame: but deal with us after thy loving kindness and according to the multitude of thy mercies. Deliver us also according to thy marvellous works, and give glory to thy name, O Lord: and let all them that do thy servant's hurt be ashamed; and let them be confounded in all their power and might, and let their strength be broken; and let them know that thou art Lord, the only God, and glorious over the whole world. " Glory be to &c."

Prayer by Priest.
Hymn of St. Isaac.
Exhortation by Deacon.

Song of the Blessed Virgin Mary, Mother of God.
St. Luke, i, 47—55.

AND my spirit hath rejoiced in God my Saviour. For he hath regarded the low estate of his handmaiden: for behold, from henceforth all generations shall call me blessed. For he that is mighty hath done to me great things; and holy is his name. And his mercy is on them that fear him from generation to generation. He hath shewed strength with his arm; he hath scattered the proud in the imagination of their hearts. He hath put down the mighty from their seats, and exalted them of low degree. He hath filled the hungry with good things; and the rich he hath sent empty away. He hath holpen his servant Israel, in remembrance of his mercy. As he spake to our fathers, to Abraham, and to his seed for ever.

Glory to the Father, etc.

———o———

Hymn of St. Isaac.
Exhortation by Deacon.
Prayer by Priest.

———o———

Psalm, li.

HAVE mercy upon me, O God, according to thy loving kindness: according unto the multitude of thy tender mercies blot out my transgressions. Wash me thoroughly from mine iniquity, and cleanse me from my sin. (See page 32).

———o———

Hymn of St. Isaac.

———o———

Psalm, cxlviii.

PRAISE ye the Lord. Praise ye the Lord from the heavens: praise him in the heights. Praise ye him, all his angels: praise ye him, all his hosts. Praise ye him, sun and moon; praise him, all ye stars of light. Praise him, ye heavens of heaven, and ye waters that be above the heavens. Let them praise the name of the Lord: for he commanded, and they were created.

―o―

Hymn of St. Isaac.

―o―

Song of the Angels and of one hundred and fifty Fathers of the Holy Council of Constantinople.

GLORY to God in the highest, and on earth peace, good will toward men. Praise be to Thee in the highest; blessed art Thou, O Lord our God; we bless and magnify Thee. We confess and worship Thee, O Lord; we glorify Thee, we thank Thee, O Lord, for Thy great glory, O Lord and King, heavenly Holiness, God and Father Almighty. O Jesus Christ our Lord, and only begotten Son of the Father. Lord God and Lamb of God; and Son of the Father, who took human nature of the Holy Virgin through Thy mercy hast taken away the sins of the world, accept our supplication; O Holy (Lord) who sittest on the right hand of the Father, have mercy upon us. For Thou art only Holy. Thou art the most high and our only

HOLY THURSDAY NIGHT.

Lord Jesus Christ. Thou art Lord O Holy Ghost in the glory of God the Father. Amen.

WE always bless Thee, Lord, and magnify Thy Holy name for ever and ever. Make us worthy O Lord to pass this day in peace and keep us without sin. Blessed art Thou Lord God of our fathers, praised and glorified is Thy Holy name for ever. Amen. O Blessed Lord teach me Thy statutes (*repeated thrice*), our dwelling place (refuge) in all generations. I beseech Thee, O Lord, have mercy upon me. Heal my soul: I have sinned against Thee; shew us Thy mercies, O Lord, and grant us Thy salvation. Thy mercy, O Lord, endureth for ever: forsake not the works of Thy own hands, O Lord. Thou art my refuge; teach me to do Thy will; for Thou art my God; for with Thee is the fountain of life: in Thy light shall we see light. O Lord continue forth thy loving kindness unto them that know Thee.

Priest: Glory, honour, and worship be to the Father and to the Son and to the Holy Ghost, now and ever world without end. Amen.

Anthem.

I AM shut up, and I cannot come forth; mine eye mourneth by reason of affliction. Lord, I have called daily upon thee; I have streched out my hands unto thee.—*Psalm, lxxxviii,* 8—9.

Litany.
Prayer by the Priest.
Trisagion.
Holy God, Holy and Mighty, Holy and Immortal, who wast betrayed for us, have mercy upon us (repeated thrice), etc.

Psalm, cxiii, 1—9. "Praise ye the Lord."
Hymn of St. Isaac.
Exhortation by Deacon.
Prayer by Priest.

———o———

Psalm, cix, 1—31. " Hold not thy peace." (See page 110.)
St. John, xviii, 28—xix, 16.

THEN led they Jesus from Caiaphas unto the hall of judgment : and it was early ; and they themselves went not into the judgment hall, lest they should be defiled, but that they might eat the passover. Pilate then went out unto them, and said, What accusation bring ye against this man ? They answered and said unto him, If he were not a malefactor, we would not have delivered him up unto thee. Then said Pilate unto them, Take ye him, and judge him according to your law. The Jews therefore said unto him, It is not lawful for us to put any man to death : that the saying of Jesus might be fulfilled, which he spake, signifying what death he should die. Then Pilate entered into the judgment hall again, and called Jesus, and said

HOLY THURSDAY NIGHT.

unto him, Art thou the King of the Jews? Jesus answered him, Sayest thou this thing of thyself, or did others tell it thee of me? Pilate answered, Am I a Jew? Thine own nation and the chief priests have delivered thee unto me: what hast thou done? Jesus answered, My kingdom is not of this world: if my kingdom were of this world, then would my servants fight, that I should not be delivered to the Jews: but now is my kingdom not from hence. Pilate therefore said unto him, Art thou a King then? Jesus answered, Thou sayest that I am a King. To this end was I born, and for this cause came I into the world, that I should bear witness unto the truth. Every one that is of the truth heareth my voice. Pilate said unto him, What is truth? And when he had said this, he went out again unto the Jews, and saith unto them, I find in him no fault at all. But ye have a custom, that I should release unto you one of the passover: will ye therefore that I release unto you the King of the Jews? Then cried they all again, saying not this man, but Barabbas. Now Barabbas was a robber. Then Pilate therefore took Jesus, and scourged him. And the soldiers platted a crown of thorns, and put it on his head, and they put on him a purple robe, and said, Hail, King of the Jews! and they smote him with their hands. Pilate went forth again and saith unto them, Behold, I bring him forth to you, that ye may know that I find no fault in him. Then came Jesus forth, wearing the crown of thorns, and the purple robe. And Pilate saith unto them, Behold the man! When the chief priests therefore and officers saw him, they cried out, saying, Crucify him, crucify him. Pilate saith unto them, Take ye him, and crucify him: for I find no fault in him. The Jews answered him, We have a law, and by our law he ought to die, because he made himself the Son of God. When Pilate therefore heard that saying, he was the more afraid; and went out again into the judgment hall, and saith unto Jesus, Whence art thou? But Jesus gave him no answer. Then saith Pilate unto him, Speakest thou not unto me? Knowest thou not that I have power to crucify thee, and have power to release thee? Jesus answered, Thou couldest have no power at all against me, except it were given thee from above: therefore he that delivered me unto thee hath the greater sin. And from thenceforth Pilate sought to release him: but the Jews cried out, saying, If thou let this man go, thou art not Cæsar's friend: whosoever maketh himself a king speaketh against Cæsar. When Pilate therefore heard that saying, he brought Jesus forth, and sat down in the judgment seat in a place that is called the Pavement, but in the Hebrew, Gabratha. And it was the preparation of the passover, and about the sixth hour: and he saith unto the Jews, Behold your King! But they cried out, Away with him, away with him, crucify him. Pilate saith unto them, Shall I crucify your King? The chief priests answered, We have no king but Cæsar. Then delivered he him therefore unto them to be crucified.

---o---

Hymn of St. Nierses.
Exhortation by the Deacon.
Prayer by the Priest.
Ceremony of the Holy Cross.

---o---

GOOD FRIDAY MORNING.

---o---

MORNING SERVICE AT 9 O'CLOCK.

Psalm, li, 1—19. "Have mercy upon me, O God." See page 53 (repeated twice with exhortations and other prayers).

---o---

Midday Service.

---o---

Psalm, xxxv, 1—28.

PLEAD my cause, O Lord, with them that strive with me: fight against them that fight against me. Take hold of shield and buckler, and stand up for mine help. Draw out also the spear, and stop the way against them that persecute me: say unto my soul, I am thy salvation. Let them be confounded and put to shame that seek after my soul: let them be turned back and brought to confusion that devise my hurt. Let them be as chaff before the wind, and let the angel of the Lord chase them. Let their way be dark and slippery: and let the angel of the Lord persecute them. For without cause have they hid for me their net in a pit, which without cause they have digged for my soul. Let destruction come upon him at unawares: and let his net that he hath hid catch him: into that very destruction let him fall. And my soul shall be joyful in the Lord: it shall rejoice in his salvation. All my bones shall say, Lord, who is like unto thee, which deliverest the poor from him that is too strong for him, yea, the poor and the needy from him that spoileth him? False witness did rise up! they laid to my charge things that I knew not. They rewarded me evil for good to the spoiling of my soul. But as for me, when they were sick, my clothing was sack cloth: I humbled my soul with fasting! and my prayer returned into my own bosom. I behaved myself as though he had been my friend or my brother: I bowed down heavily, as one that mourneth for his mother. But in mine adversity they rejoiced and gathered themselves together: yea, abjects gathered themselves together against me, and I knew it not! they did tear me and cease not. With hypocritical mockers in feasts, they gnashed upon me with their teeth. Lord, how long wilt thou look on? Rescue my soul from their destructions, my darling from the lions. I will give thee thanks in the great congregation : I will praise thee among much people. Let not them that are mine enemies wrongfully rejoice over me: neither let them wink with the eye that hath me without a cause. For they speak not peace: but they devise deceitful matters against them that are quiet in the land. Yea, they opened their mouth wide against me, and said, Aha, aha, our eye hath seen it. These thou hast seen, O Lord! keep not silence : O Lord, be not far from me. Stir up thyself, and awake to my judgment, even unto my cause, my God and my Lord. Judge me, O Lord my God, according to thy righteousness! and let them not rejoice over me. Let them not say in their hearts, Ah, so would we have it : let them not say, We have swallowed him. Let them be ashamed and brought to confusion together that rejoice at mine hurt : let them be clothed with shame and dishonour that magnify themselves against me. Let them shout for joy, and be glad, that favour my righteous cause : yea, let them say continually, Let the Lord be magnified which hath pleasure in the prosperity of his servant.

AND my tongue shall speak of thy righteousness and of thy praise all the day long.

Zechariah, xi, 11—14.

AND it was broken in that day : and so the poor of the flock that waited upon me knew that it was the word of the Lord. And I said unto them, If he think good, give me my price; and if not, forbear. So they weighed for my price thirty pieces of silver. And the Lord said unto me, Cast it unto the potter: a goodly price that I was prised at of them. And I took the thirty pieces of silver, and cast them to the potter in the house of the Lord. Then I cut asunder mine other staff, even bands, that I might break the brotherhood between Judah and Israel.

Galatians, vi, 14---18.

BUT God forbid that I should glory, save in the cross of our Lord Jesus Christ, by whom the world is crucified unto me, and I unto the world. For in Christ Jesus neither circumcision availeth anything, nor uncircumcision, but a new creature; and as many as walk according to this rule, peace be on them, and mercy, and upon the Israel of God. From henceforth let no man trouble me; for I bear in my body the marks of the Lord Jesus. Brethren, the grace of our Lord Jesus Christ be with your spirit. Amen.

Litany.

―o―

Prayers by the Priest.

Psalm, xxxviii, 1—22.

O LORD, rebuke me not in thy wrath, neither chasten me in thy hot displeasure. For thine arrows stick fast in me, and thy hand presseth me sore. There is no soundness in my flesh because of thine anger; neither is there any rest in my bones because of my sin. For mine iniquities are gone over mine head; as an heavy burden they are too heavy for me. My wounds stink and are corrupt because of my foolishness. I am troubled; I am bowed down greatly; I go mourning all the day long. For my loins are filled with a lothsome disease: and there is no soundness in my flesh. I am feeble and sore broken: I have roared by reason of the disquietness of my heart. Lord, all my desire is before thee; and my groaning is not hid from thee. My heart panteth, my strength faileth me: as for the light of mine eyes, it also is gone from me. My lovers and my friends stand aloof from my sore; and my kinsmen stand afar off. They also that seek after my life lay snares for me: and they that seek my hurt speak mischievous things, and imagine deceits all the day long. But I, as a deaf man, heard not; and I was as a dumb man that openeth not his mouth. Thus I was a man that heareth not, and in whose mouth are no reproofs. For in thee, O Lord, do I hope: thou wilt hear, O Lord my God. For I said, Hear me, lest otherwise they should rejoice over me: when my foot slippeth, they magnify themselves against me. For I am ready to halt, and my sorrow is continually before me. For I will declare mine iniquity; I will be sorry for my sin. But mine enemies are lively, and they are strong: and they that hate me wrongfully are multiplied. They also that render evil for good are mine adversaries; because I follow the thing that good is, forsake me not, O Lord: O my God, be not far from me. Make haste to help me, O Lord my salvation.

Isaiah, iii, 9—15.

THE shew of their countenance doth witness against them; and they declare their sin as Sodom; they hide it not. Woe unto their souls! for they have rewarded evil unto themselves. Say ye to the righteous, that it shall be well with him: for they shall eat the fruit of their doings. Woe unto the wicked! it shall be ill with him: for the reward of his hands shall be given him. As for my people, children are their oppresors, and women rule over them. O my people, they which lead thee cause thee to err, and destroy the way of thy paths. The Lord standeth up to plead, and standeth to judge the people. The Lord will enter into judgment with the ancients of his people, and the princes thereof: for ye have eaten up the vineyard; the spoil of the poor is in your houses. What mean ye that ye beat my people to pieces, and grind the faces of the poor? saith the Lord God of hosts.

Philippians, ii, 5—11.

LET this mind be in you, which was also in Christ Jesus: who, being in the form of God, thought it not robbery to be equal with God: but made himself of no reputation, and took upon him the form of a servant, and was made in the likeness of men. And being found in fashion as a man, he humbled himself, and became obedient unto death, even the death of the cross. Wherefore God also hath highly exalted him, and given him a name which is above every man: that at the name of Jesus every knee should bow, of things in heaven, and things in earth, and things under the earth; and that every tongue should confess that Jesus Christ is Lord, to the glory of God the Father.

Litany.

———o———

Prayers by the Priest.

———o———

Psalm, xli, 1—13.

BLESSED is he that considereth the poor: the Lord will deliver him in the time of trouble. The Lord will preserve him, and keep him alive; and he shall be blessed upon the earth: and thou wilt not deliver him unto the will of his enemies. The Lord will strengthen him upon the bed of languishing: thou wilt make all his bed in his sickness. I said, Lord, be merciful unto me; heal my soul; for I have sinned against thee. Mine enemies speak evil of me, When shall he die, and his name perish? And if he come to see me, he speaketh vanity: his heart gathereth iniquity to itself; when he goeth abroad, he telleth it. All that hate me whisper together against me: against me do they devise my hurt. An evil disease, say they, cleaveth fast unto him: and now that he lieth he shall rise up no more. Yea, mine own familiar friend, in whom I trusted, which did eat of my bread, hath lifted up his heel against me. But thou, O Lord, be merciful unto me, and raise me up, that I may requite them. By this I know that thou favourest me, because mine enemy doth not triumph over me. And as for me, thou upholdese me in mine integrity, and settest me before thy fact for ever. Blessed be the Lord God of Israel from everlasting, and to everlasting. Amen and Amen.

Isaiah, l, 4—9.

THE LORD GOD hath given me the tongue of the learned, that I should know how to speak a word in season to him that is weary: he wakeneth morning by morning, he wakeneth mine ear to hear as the learned. The Lord God hath opened mine ear, and I was not rebellious, neither turn away back. I gave my back to the smiters, and my cheeks to them that plucked off the hair: I hid not my face from shame and spitting. For the Lord God will help me; therefore shall I not be confounded: therefore have I set my face like a flint, and I know that I shall not be ashamed. He is near that justifieth me! Who will contend with me? Let us stand together: who is mine adversary? Let him come near to me. Behold, the Lord God will help me! Who is he that shall condemn me?

Romans, v, 6—11.

FOR when we were yet without strength, in due time Christ died for the ungodly. For scarcely for a righteous man will one die: yet peradventure for a good man some would even dare to die. But God commendeth his love toward us, in that, while we were yet sinners, Christ died for us. Much more then, being now justified by his blood, we shall be saved from wrath through him. For if, when we were enemies, we were reconciled to God by the death of his Son, much more, being reconciled, we shall be saved by his life.

And not only so, but we also joy in God through our Lord Jesus Christ, by whom we have now received the atonement.

Litany.

———o———

Prayer by the Priest.

———o———

Psalm, xxii, 1—31.

MY GOD, my God, why hast thou forsaken me? Why art thou so far from helping me, and from the words of my roaring? O my God, I cry in the daytime, but thou hearest not; and in the night season, and am not silent. But thou art holy, O thou that inhabitest the praises of Israel. Our fathers trusted in thee; they trusted, and thou didst deliver them. They cried unto thee, and were delivered: they trusted in thee, and were not confounded. But I am a worm, and no man! a reproach of men, and despise of the people. All they that see me laugh me to scorn: they shoot out the lip, they shake the head, saying, He trusted on the Lord that he would deliver him: let him deliver him, seeing he delighted in him. But thou art he that took me out of the womb; thou didst make me hope when I was upon my mother's breast. I was cast upon thee from the womb: thou art my God from my mother's belly. Be not far from me; for trouble is near; for there is none to help. Many bulls have compassed me; strong bulls of Bashan have beset me round. They gaped upon me with their mouths, as a raving and a roaring lion. I am poured out like water, and all my bones are out of joint: my heart is like wax; it is melted in the midst of my bowels. My strength is dried up like a potsherd; and my tongue cleaveth to my jaws; and thou hast brought me into the dust of death. For dogs have compassed me: the assembly of the wicked have enclosed me: they pierced my hands and my feet. I may tell all my bones: they look and stare upon me. They part my garments among them, and cast lots upon my vesture. But be not thou far from me, O Lord: O my strength, haste thee to help me. Deliver my soul from the sword; my darling from the power of the dog. Save me from the lion's mouth: for thou hast heard me from the horns of the unicorns. I will declare thy name unto my brethren: in the midst of the congregation will I praise thee. Ye that fear the Lord, praise him; all ye the seed of Jacob, glorify him; and fear him all ye the seed of Israel. For he hath not despised nor abhorred the affliction of the afflicted: neither hath he hid his face from him; but when he cried unto him, he heard. My praise shall be of thee in the great congregation: I will pay my vows before them that fear him. The meek shall eat and be satisfied: they shall praise the Lord that seek him: your heart shall live for ever. All the ends of the world shall remember and turn unto the Lord: and all the kindreds of the nations shall worship before thee. For the kingdom is the Lord's: and he is the governor among the nations. All they that be fat upon earth shall eat and worship: all they that go down to the dust shall bow before him: and none can keep alive his own soul. A seed shall serve him; it shall be accounted to the Lord for a generation. They shall come, and shall declare his righteousness unto a people that shall be born, that he hath done this.

———o———

Amos, viii, 9—12.

AND it shall come to pass in that day, saith the Lord God, that I will cause the sun to go down at noon, and I will darken the earth in the clear day: and I will turn your feasts into mourning, and all your songs into lamentation; and I will bring up sackcloth upon all loins, and baldness upon every head; and I will make it as the mourning of an only son, and the end thereof as a bitter day. Behold, the days come, saith the Lord, that I will send a famine in the land, not a famine of bread, nor a thirst for water, but of hearing the words of the Lord: and they shall wander from sea to sea, and from the north, even to the east, they shall run to and fro to seek the word of the Lord, and shall not find it.

I Corinthians, i, 18—31.

FOR the preaching of the cross is to them that perish foolishness! but unto us which are saved it is the power of God. For it is written, I will destroy the wisdom of the wise, and will bring to nothing the understanding of the prudent. Where is the wise? Where is the scribe? Where is the disputer of this world? Hath not God made foolish the wisdom of this world? For after that in the wisdom of God the world by wisdom knew not God, it pleased God by the foolishness of preaching to save them that believe. For the Jews require a sign, and the Greeks seek after wisdom : but we preach Christ crucified, unto the Jews a stumbling block, and unto the Greeks foolishness. But unto them which are called, both Jews and Greeks, Christ the power of God, and the wisdom of God, because the foolishness of God is wiser than men, and the weakness of God stronger than men. For ye see your calling, brethren, how that not many wise men after the flesh, not many mighty, not many noble, are called : but God hath chosen the foolish things of the world to confound the wise! and God hath chosen the weak things of the world to confound the things which are mighty! And base things of the world, and things which are despised, hath God chosen, yea, and things which are not, to bring to nought things that are : that no flesh should glory in his presence. But of him are ye in Christ Jesus, who of God is made unto us wisdom, and righteousness, and sanctification, and redemption : that, according as it is written, He that glorieth, let him glory in the Lord.

Litany.

— o —

Psalm, xxxi, 1—24.

IN thee, O Lord, do I put my trust : let me never be ashamed : deliver me in thy righteousness. Bow down thine ear to me; deliver me speedily : be thou my strong rock, for an house of defence to save me. For thou, art my rock and my fortress; therefore for thy names sake lead me and guide me. Pull me out of the net that they have laid privily for me; for thou art my strength. Into thine hand I commit my spirit: thou hast redeemed me, O Lord God of truth. I have hated them that regard lying vanities; but I trust in the Lord. I will be glad and rejoice in thy mercy: for thou hast considered my trouble; thou hast known my soul in adversaries; and hast not shut me up into the hand of the enemy: thou hast set my feet in a large room. Have mercy upon me, O Lord, for I am in trouble: mine eye is consumed with grief, yea, my soul and my belly. For my life is spent with grief, and my years with sighing; my strength faileth because of mine iniquity, and my bones are consumed. I was a reproach among all mine enemies, but especially among my neighbours, and a fear to mine acquaintance: they that didst see me without fled from me. I am forgotten as a dead man out of mind; I am like a broken vessel. For I have heard the slander of many: fear was on every side: while they took counsel together against me; they devised to take away my life. But I trusted in thee, O Lord: I saith, Thou art my God. My times are in thy hand: deliver me from the hand of mine enemies, and from them that persecute me. Make thy face to shine upon thy servant: save me for thy mercies' sake. Let me not be ashamed, O Lord; for I have called upon thee: let the wicked be ashamed, and let them be silent in the grave. Let the lying lips be put to silence; which speak grievous things proudly and contemptuously against the righteous. O how great is thy goodness, which thou hast laid me for them that fear thee; which thou hast wrought for them that trust in thee before the sons of men! Thou shalt hide them in the secret of thy presence from the pride of man: thou shalt keep them secretly in a pavilion from the strife of tongues. Blessed be the Lord: for he hath shewed me his marvellous kindness in a strong city. For I said in my haste, I am cut off from before thine eyes: nevertheless thou heardst the voice of my supplications when I cried unto thee. O love the Lord, all ye his saints: for the Lord preserved the faithful, and plentifully rewardeth the proud doer. Be of good courage, and he shall strengthen your heart, all ye that hope in the Lord.

Isaiah, lii 13—liii, 12.

BEHOLD, my servant shall deal prudently; he shall be exalted and extolled, and be very high, as many were astonied at thee; his visage was so marred more than any man, and his form more than the sons of men. So shall he sprinkle many nations; the kings shall shut their mouths at him: for that which hath not been told them shall they see; and that which they had not heard shall they consider. Who hath believed our report ? and to whom is the arm of the Lord revealed ? For he shall grow up before him as a tender plant, and as a root out of a dry ground : he hath no form nor comeliness ; and when we shall see him, there is no beauty that we should desire him. He is despised and rejected of men ; a man of sorrows, and acquainted with grief : and we hid as it were our faces from him ; he was despised, and we esteemed him not. Surely he hath borne our griefs, and carried our sorrows : yet we did esteem him stricken, smitten of God, and afflicted. But he was wounded for our trangressions ; he was bruised for our iniquities ; the chastisement of our peace was upon him ; and with his stripes we are healed. All we like sheep have gone away ; we have turned every one to his own way ; and the Lord hath laid on him the iniquity of us all. He was oppressed, and he was afflicted, yet he opened not his mouth : he is brought as a lamb to the slaughter ; and as a sheep before her shearers is dumb, so he openeth not his mouth. He was taken from prison and from judgment : and who shall declare his generation ? For he was cut off out of the land of the living ; for the transgression of my people was he stricken, And he made his grave with the wicked, and with the rich in his death ; because he hath done no violence, neither was any deceit in his mouth. Yet it pleased the Lord to bruise him ;

he hath put him to grief; when thou shalt make his soul and offering for sin, he shall see his seed; he shall prolong his days, and the pleasure of the Lord shall prosper in his hand. He shall see of the travail of his soul, and shall be satisfied: by his knowledge shall my righteous servant justify many; for he shall bear their iniquities. Therefore will I divide him a portion with the great, and he shall divide the spoil with the strong; because he hath poured out his soul unto death: and he was numbered with the transgressors; and he bare the sin of many, and made intercession for the transgressors.

Hebrews, ii, 11—18.

FOR both he that sanctifieth and they who are sanctified are all of one: for which cause he is not ashamed to call them brethren saying, I will declare thy name unto my brethren, in the midst of the church will I sing praise unto thee. And again, I will put my trust in him. and again, behold I and the children which God hath given me. Forasmuch then as the children are partakers of flesh and blood, he also himself likewise took part of the same; that through death he might destroy him that at the power of death, that is, the devil; And deliver them who through fear of death were all their lifetime subject to bondage. For verily he took not on him the nature of angels; but he took on him the seed of Abraham.

Wherefore in all things it behoved him to be made like unto his brethren, that he might be a merciful and faithful high priest in things pertaining to God, to make reconciliation for the sins of the people. For in that he himself hath suffered being tempted, he is able to succour them that are tempted.

Hymn of St. Nierses the Graceful.

—o—

St. Matthew, xxvii, 1—56.

WHEN the morning was come, all the chief priests and elders of the people took counsel against Jesus to put him to death: and when they had bound him, they led him away, and delivered him to Pontius Pilate, the governor. Then Judas, which had betrayed him, when he saw that he was condemned, repented himself, and brought again the thirty pieces of silver to the chief priests and elders, saying, I have sinned in that I have betrayed the innocent blood. And they said, What is that to us? See thou to that. And he cast down the pieces of silver in the temple, and departed, and went and hanged himself. And the chief priests took the silver pieces, and said, It is not lawful for to put them into the treasury, because it is the price of blood. And they took counsel, and bought with them the potter's field, to bury strangers in. Wherefore that field was called, The field of blood, unto this day. Then was fulfilled that which was spoken by Jeremy, the prophet, saying, And they took the thirty pieces of silver, the price of him that was valued, whom they of the children of Israel did value; and gave them for the potter's field, as the Lord appointed me. And Jesus stood before the governor: and the governor asked him, saying, Art thou the king of the Jews? And Jesus said unto him, Thou sayest. And when he was accused of the chief priests and elders, he answered nothing. Then said Pilate unto him, Hearest thou not how many things they witness against thee? And he answered him to never a word; inasmuch that the governor marvelled greatly. Now at that feast the governor was wont to release unto the people a prisoner, whom they would. And they had then a notable prisoner, called Barabbas. Therefore when they were gathered together, Pilate said unto them, Whom will ye that I release unto you? Barabbas, or Jesus which is called Christ? For he knew that for envy they had delivered him. When he was set down on the judgment seat, his wife sent unto him, saying, Have thou nothing to do with that just man: for I have suffered many things this day in a dream because of him. But the chief priests and elders persuaded the multitude that they should ask Barabbas, and destroy Jesus. The Governor answered and said unto them, Whether of the twain will ye that I release unto you? They said, Barabbas. Pilate saith unto them, What shall I do then with Jesus which is called Christ? They all say unto him, Let him be crucified. And the Governor said, Why, what evil hath he done? But they cried out the more, saying, Let him be crucified. When Pilate saw that he could prevail nothing, but that rather a tumult was made, he took water, and washed his hands before the multitude, saying, I am innocent of the blood of this just person: see ye to it. Then answered all the people, and said, His blood be on us, and on our children. Then released he Barabbas unto them: and when he had scourged Jesus, he delivered him to be crucified. Then the soldiers of the Governor took Jesus into the common hall, and gathered unto him the whole band of soldiers. And they stripped him, and put on him a scarlet robe. And when they had platted a crown of thorns, they put it upon his head, and a reed in his right hand: and they bowed the knee before him, and mocked him, saying, Hail, King of the Jews! And they spit upon him, and took the reed, and smote him on the head. And after that they had mocked him, they took the robe off from him, and put his own raiment on him, and led him away to crucify him, And as they came out they found a man of Cyrene, Simon by name; him they compelled to bear his cross. And when they were come unto a place called Golgotha, that is to say, a place of a skull, they gave him vinegar to drink mingled with gall: and when he had tasted thereof, he would not drink. And they crucified him, and parted his garments, casting lots: that it might be fulfilled which was spoken by the prophet, They parted my garments among them, and upon my vesture did they cast lots. And sitting down they watched him there; and set up over his head his accusation written, This is Jesus the King of the Jews. Then were there two thieves crucified with him, one on the right hand, and another on the left. And they that passed by reviled him, wagging their heads, and saying, Thou that destroyest the temple and buildest it in three days save thyself. If thou be the Son of God, come down from the cross. Likewise also the chief priests mocking him, with the scribes and elders, said, He saved others; himself he cannot save. If he be the King of Israel, let him now come down from the cross, and we will believe him. He trusted in God; let him deliver him now, if he will have him: for he said, I am the Son of God. The thieves also, which were crucified with him, cast the same in his teeth. Now from the sixth hour there was darkness over all the land unto the ninth hour. And about the ninth hour Jesus cried with a loud voice, saying, Eli, Eli, lama sabacthani? this is to say, My God, my God, why hast thou forsaken me? Some of them that stood there, when they heard that, said, This man calleth for Elias. And straightway one of them ran, and took a sponge, and filled it with vinegar, and put it on a reed, and gave him to drink. The rest said, Let be; let us see whether Elias will come to save him. Jesus, when he had cried again with a loud voice, yielded up the ghost. And, behold, the veil of the temple was rent in twain from the top to the bottom; and the earth did quake, and the rocks rent; and the graves were opened; and many bodies of the saints which slept arose, and came out of the graves after his resurrection, and went into the holy city, and appeared unto many. Now when the centurion, and they that were with him, watching Jesus saw the earthquake, and those things that were done, they feared greatly, saying, Truly this was the Son of God. And many women were there beholding afar off, which followed Jesus from Galilee, ministering unto him: among which was Mary Magdalene, and Mary the mother of James and Joses, and the mother of Zebedee's children.

Litany.

—o—

Psalm, lxix, 1—36.

SAVE me, O God: for the waters are come in unto my soul. I sink in deep mire, where there is no standing: I am come into deep waters, where the floods overflow me. I am weary of my crying; my throat is dried: mine eyes fail while I wait for my God. They that hate me without a cause are more than the hairs of mine head; they that would destroy me, being mine enemies wrongfully, are mighty: then I restored that which I took not away. O God, thou knowest my foolishness; and my sins are not hid from thee. Let not them that wait on thee, O Lord God of hosts, be ashamed for my sake; let not those that seek thee be confounded for my sake, O God of Israel. Because for thy sake I have borne reproach; shame hath covered my face. I am become a stranger unto my brethren, and an alien unto my mother's children. For the zeal of thine house hath eaten me up: and the reproaches of them that reproached thee are fallen upon me. When I wept, and chastened my soul with fasting, that was to my reproach. I made sackcloth also my garment; and I became a proverb to them. They that sit in the gate speak against me; and I was the song of the drunkards. But as for me, my prayer is unto thee, O Lord, in an acceptable time: O God, in the multitude of thy mercy, hear me in the truth of thy salvation. Deliver me out of the mire, and let me not sink? Let me be delivered from them that hate me, and out of the deep waters. Let not the waterflood overflow me; neither let the deep swallow me up; and let not the pit shut her mouth upon me. Hear me, O Lord; for thy loving kindness is good: turn unto me according to the multitude of thy tender mercies. And hide not thy face from thy servant; for I am in trouble: hear me speedily. Draw nigh unto my soul, and redeem it: deliver me because of mine enemies. Thou hast known my reproach, and my shame, and my dishonour; mine adversaries are all before thee. Reproach hath broken my heart; and I am full of heaviness: and I looked for some to take pity, but there was none; and for comforters, but I found none. They gave me also gall for my meat; and in my thirst they gave me vinegar to drink. Let their table become a snare before them: and that which should have been for their welfare, let it become a trap. Let their eyes be darkened, that they see not; and make their loins continually to shake. Pour out thine indignation upon them, and let thy wrathful anger take hold of them. Let their habitation be desolate; and let none dwell in their tents. For they persecute him whom thou hast smitten; and they talk to the grief of those whom thou hast wounded. Add iniquity unto their iniquity; and let them not come into thy righteousness. Let them be blotted out of the blood of the living, and not be written with the righteous. But I am poor and sorrowful: let thy salvation, O God, set me up on high. I will praise the name of God with a song, and will magnify him with thanksgiving. This also shall please the Lord better than an ox or bullock that hath horns and hoofs. The humble shall see this and be glad: and your heart shall live that seek God. For the Lord heareth the poor, and despiseth not his prisoners. Let the heaven and earth praise him, the seas, and everything that moveth therein. For God will save Zion, and will build the cities of Judah that they might dwell there, and have it in possession. The seed also of his servants shall inherit it, and they that love his name shall dwell therein.

Isaiah, lxiii, 1—6.

WHO is this that cometh from Edom, with dyed garments from Bozrah? This that is glorious in his apparel, travelling in the greatness of his strength. I that speak in righteousness, mighty to save. Wherefore art thou red in thine apparel, and thy garments like him that treadeth in the wine fat? I have trodden the winepress alone; and of the people there was none with me: for I will tread them in mine anger, and trample them in my fury: and their blood shall be sprinkled upon my garments, and I will stain all my raiment. For the day of vengeance is in mine heart, and the year of my redeemed is come. And I looked, and there was none to help; and I wondered that there was none to uphold: therefore mine own arm brought salvation unto me; and my fury, it upheld me. And I will tread down the people in mine anger, and make them drunk in my fury, and I will bring down their strength to the earth.

—o—

Hebrews, ix, 11—28.

BUT Christ being come an high priest of good things to come, by a greater and more perfect tabernacle, not made with hands, that is to say, not of this building; neither by the blood of goats and calves, but by his own blood he entered in once into the holy place, having obtained eternal redemption for us. For if the blood of bulls and of goats, and the ashes of an heifer sprinkling the unclean, sanctifieth to the purifying of the flesh, how much more shall the blood of Christ, who through the eternal spirit offered himself without spot to God, purge your conscience from dead works to serve the living God? And for this cause he is the mediator of the new testament, that by means of death, for the redemption of the transgressions that were under the first testament, they which are called might receive the promise of eternal inheritance. For where a testament is, there must also of necessity be the death of the testator. For a testament is of force after men are dead, otherwise it is of no strength at all while the testator liveth. Whereupon neither the first testament was dedicated without blood. For when Moses had spoken every precept to all the people according to the law, he took the blood of calves and of goats, with water, and scarlet wool, and hyssop, and sprinkled both the book, and all the people, saying, This is the blood of the testament which God hath enjoined unto you. Moreover he sprinkled with blood both the tabernacle, and all the vessels of the ministry. And almost all things are by the law purged with blood; and without shedding of blood is no remission. It was therefore necessary that the patterns of things in the heavens should be purified with these; but the heavenly things themselves with better sacrifices than these. For Christ is not entered into the holy places made with hands, which are the figures of the true; but into heaven itself now to appear in the presence of God for us: nor yet that he should offer himself often, as the high priest entereth into the holy place every year with blood of others. For then must he often have suffered since the foundation of the world: but now once in the end of the world hath he appeared to put away sin by the sacrifice of himself. And as it is appointed unto men once to die, but after this the judgment, so Christ was once offered to bear the sins of many; and unto them that look for him shall he appear the second time without sin unto salvation.

Hymn of St. Nierses the Graceful.

St. Mark, xv, 1—41.

AND straightway in the morning the chief priests held a consultation with the elders and scribes and the whole council, and bound Jesus, and carried him away, and delivered him to Pilate. And Pilate asked him,

Art thou the King of the Jews? And he answering said unto him, Thou sayest it. And the chief priests accused him of many things: but he answered nothing. And Pilate asked him again, saying, Answerest thou nothing? Behold how many things they witness against thee. But Jesus yet answered nothing; so that Pilate marvelled. Now at that feast he released unto them one prisoner, whomsoever they desired. And there was one named Barabbas, which lay bound with them that had made insurrection with him, who had committed murder in the insurrection. And the multitude crying aloud began to desire him to do as he had ever done unto them. But Pilate answered them, saying, Will ye that I release unto you the King of the Jews? For he knew that the chief priests had delivered him for envy. But the chief priests moved the people, that he should rather release Barabbas unto them. And Pilate answered and said again unto them, What will ye then that I shall do unto him whom ye call the King of the Jews? And they cried out again, Crucify him. Then Pilate said unto them, Why, what evil hath he done? And they cried out the more exceedingly, Crucify him. And so Pilate, willing to content the people, released Barabbas unto them, and delivered Jesus, when he had scourged him, to be crucified. And the soldiers led him away into the hall, called Praetorium; and they called together the whole band. And they clothed him with purple, and platted a crown of thorns, and put it about his head. And began to salute him, Hail King of the Jews! And they smote him on the head with a reed, and did spit upon him, and bowing their knees worshipped him. And when they had mocked him, they took off the purple from him, and put his own clothes on him, and led him out to crucify him. And they compel one Simon, a Cyrenian, who passed by, coming out of the country, the father of Alexander and Rufus, to bear his cross. And they bring him unto the place Golgotha, which is, being interpreted, The place of a skull. And they gave him to drink wine mingled with myrrh: but he received it not. And when they had crucified him, they parted his garments, casting lots upon them, what every man should take. And it was the third hour, and they crucified him. And the superscription of his accusation was written over, The King of the Jews. And with him they crucify two thieves; the one on his right hand, and the other on his left. And the scripture was fulfilled, which saith, And he was numbered with the transgressors. And they that passed by railed on him, wagging their heads, and saying, Ah, thou that destroyest the temple, and buildest it in three days, save thyself, and come down from the cross. Likewise also the chief priests mocking said among themselves with the scribes, He saved others; himself he cannot save. Let Christ the King of

Israel descend now from the cross that we may see and believe. And they that were crucified with him reviled him. And when the sixth hour was come, there was darkness over the whole land until the ninth hour. And at the ninth hour Jesus cried with a loud voice, saying, Eli, Eli, lama sabachthani; which is, being interpreted, My God, my God, why hast thou forsaken me? And some of them that stood by, when they heard it, said, Behold, he calleth Elias. And one of them ran and filled a sponge full of vinegar, and put it on a reed, and gave him to drink, saying, Let alone; let us see whether Elias will come to take him down. And Jesus cried with a loud voice, and gave up the ghost. And veil of the temple was rent in twain from the top to the bottom. And when the Centurion, which stood over against him, saw that he so cried out, and gave up the ghost, he said, Truly this man was the Son of God. There were also women looking on afar off: among whom was Mary Magdalene, and Mary the mother of James the less and of Joses, and Salome (who also, when he was in Galilee, followed him, and ministered unto him); and many other women which came up with him unto Jerusalem.

Psalm, cii, 1—28.

HEAR my prayer, O Lord, and let my cry come unto thee. Hide not thy face from me in the day when I am in trouble; incline thine ear unto me: in the day when I call answer me speedily. For my days are consumed like smoke, and by bones are burnt as an hearth. My heart is smitten, and withered like grass; so that I forget to eat my bread. By reason of the voice of my groaning my bones cleave to my skin. I am like a pelican of the wilderness: I am like an owl of the desert. I watch, and am as a sparrow alone upon the housetop. Mine enemies reproach me all the day; and they that are mad against me are sworn against me. For I have eaten ashes like bread, and mingled my drink with weeping, because of thine indignation and thy wrath: for thou hast lifted me up, and cast me down. My days are like a shadow that declineth; and I am withered like grass. But thou, O Lord, shall endure for ever; and thy remembrance unto all generations. Thou shalt arise, and have mercy upon Zion: for the time to favour her, yea, the set time, is come. For thy servants take pleasure in her stones, and favour the dust thereof. So the heathen shall fear the name of the Lord, and all the kings of the earth thy glory. When the Lord shall build up Zion, he shall appear in his glory. He will regard the prayer of destitute, and not despise their prayer. This shall be written for the generations to come: and the people which shall be created shall praise the Lord. For he hath looked down from the height of his sanctuary; from heaven did the Lord behold the earth; to hear the groaning of the prisoner; to loose those that are appointed to death; to declare the name of the Lord in Zion and his praise in Jerusalem; when the people are gathered together, and the kingdoms, to serve the Lord. He weakened my strength in the way; he shortened my days. I said, O my God, take me not away in the midst of my days; thy years are throughout all generations. Of old hast thou laid the foundation of the earth: and the heavens are the works of thy hands. They shall perish, but thou shalt endure, yea, all of them shall wax old like a garment; as a vesture shalt thou change them, and they shall be changed. But thou art the same, and thy years shall have no end. The children of thy servants shall continue, and their need shall be established before thee.

Jeremiah, xi, 18—xii, 8.

AND the Lord hath given me knowledge of it, and I know it; then thou shewedst me their doings. But was like a lamb or an ox that is brought to the slaughter; and I knew not that they had devised devices against me, saying, Let us destroy the tree with the fruit thereof, and let us cut him off from the land of the living, that his name may be no more remembered. But, O Lord of hosts, that judgest righteously, that triest the reins and the heart, let me see thy vengeance of them: for unto thee have I revealed my cause. Therefore thus saith the Lord of the men of Anathoth that seek thy life, saying, Prophesy not in the name of the Lord, that thou die not by our hand. Therefore thus saith the Lord of hosts, Behold, I will punish them: the young men shall die by the sword; their sons and their daughters shall die by famine; and there shall be no remnant of them: for I will bring evil upon the men of Anathoth, even the year of their visitation. Righteous art thou, O Lord, when I plead with thee: yet let me talk with thee of thy judgments. Wherefore doth the way of the wicked prosper? Wherefore are all they happy that deal very treacherously? Thou hast planted them, yea, they have taken root: they grow, yea, they bring forth fruit: thou art near in their mouth, and far from their reins. But thou O Lord, knowest me: thou hast seen me, and tried mine heart toward thee: pull them out like sheep for the slaughter, and prepare them for the day of slaughter. How long shall the land mourn, and the herbs of every field wither, for the wickedness of them that dwell therein? Beasts are consumed, and the birds; because they said, He shall not see our last end. If thou hast run with the footmen, and they have wearied thee, then how canst thou contend with horses? And if in the land of peace, wherein thou trustedst, they wearied thee, then how wilt thou do in the swelling of Jordan? For even thy brethren, and the house of thy father, even they have dealt treacherously with thee; yea, they have called a multitude after thee:

believe them not, though they speak fair words unto thee I have forsaken mine house; I have left mine heritage; I have given the dearly beloved of my soul into the hand of her enemies. Mine heritage is unto me as a lion in the forest; it crieth out against me; therefore have I hated it.

Hebrews, x, 19—31. " *Having therefore.*" (*See page* 35.)
Hymn of St. Nierses the Graceful.

———o———

St. Luke, xxii, 66—*xxiii,* 49.

AND as soon as it was day, the elders of the people and the chief priests and the scribes came together, and led him into their council, saying, Art thou the Christ? Tell us. And he said unto them, If I tell you ye will not believe: and if I also ask you, ye will not answer me nor let me go. Hereafter shall the Son of man sit on the right hand of the power of God. Then said they all, Art thou then the Son of God? And he said unto them, ye say that I am. And they said, What need we any further witness? for we ourselves have heard of his own mouth. And the whole multitude of them arose, and led him unto Pilate. And they began to accuse him, saying, We found this fellow perverting the nation, and forbidding to give tribute to Caesar, saying that he himself is Christ a King. And Pilate asked him, saying, Art thou the King of the Jews? And he answered him and said, Thou sayest it. Then said

Pilate to the chief priests and to the people, I find no fault in this man. And they were the more fierce, saying, He stirreth up the people, teaching throughout all journey, beginning from Galilee to this place. When Pilate heard of Galilee, he asked whether the man were a Galilean. And as soon as he knew that he belonged unto Herod's jurisdiction, he sent him to Herod, who himself also was at Jerusalem at that time. And when Herod saw Jesus, he was exceeding glad: for he was desirous to see him of a long season; because he had heard many things of him: and he hoped to have seen some miracles done by him. Then he questioned with him in many words; but he answered him nothing. And the chief priest and scribes stood and vehemently accused him. And Herod with his men of war set him at nought; and mocked him, and arrayed him in a gorgeous robe, and sent him again to Pilate. And the same day Pilate and Herod were made friends together: for before they were at enmity between themselves. And Pilate when he had called together the chief priests and the rulers and the people, said unto them, Ye have brought this man unto me, as one that perverteth the people: and behold, I, having examined him before you, have found no fault in this man touching those things whereof ye accuse him. No, nor yet Herod: for I sent you to him; and, lo, nothing worthy of death is done unto him. I will therefore chastise him, and release him. (For of necessity he must release one unto them at the feast.) And they cried out all at once, saying, Away with this man, and release unto us Barabbas (who for a certain sedition made in the city, and for murder, was cast into prison). Pilate therefore, willing to release Jesus, spake again to them. But they cried, saying, Crucify him, crucify him. And he said unto them the third time, Why, what evil hath he done? I have found no cause of death in him; I will therefore chastise him, and let him go, and they were instant with loud voices, requiring that he might be crucified. And the voices of them and of the chief priests prevailed. And Pilate gave sentence that it should be as they required. And he released unto them him that for sedition and murder was cast into prison, whom they had desired; but he delivered Jesus to their will. And as they led him away, they laid hold upon one Simon, a Cyrenian, coming out of the country, and on him they laid the cross, that he might bear it after Jesus. And there followed him a great company of people, and of women, which also bewailed and lamented him. But Jesus turning unto them said, Daughters of Jerusalem, weep not for me, but weep for yourselves, and for your children. For behold the days are coming, in the which they shall say, Blessed are the barren, and the wombs that never bare and the paps which never gave suck. Then shall they begin to say to the mountains, Fall on us; and to the hills cover us. For if they do these things in a green tree, what shall be done in the dry? And there were also two other, malefactors, led with him to be put to death. And when they were come to the place, which is called Calvary, there they crucified him, and the malefactors, one on the right hand and the other on the left. Then said Jesus, Father, forgive them; for they know not what they do. And they parted his raiment, and cast lots. And the people stood beholding. And the rulers also with them derided him, saying He saved others; let him save himself if he be Christ, the chosen of God. And the soldiers also mocked him, coming to him, and offering him vinegar, and saying, If thou be the King of the Jews, save thyself. And a superscription also was written over him in letters of Greek and Latin, and Hebrew, This is the King of the Jews. And one of the malefactors which were hanged railed on him, saying, If thou be the Christ, save thyself and us. But the other answering rebuked him, saying, Dost not thou fear God, seeing thou art in the same condemnation? And we indeed justly, for we receive the due reward of our deeds: but this man hath done nothing amiss. And he said unto Jesus, Lord, remember me when thou comest into thy kingdom. And Jesus said unto him, Verily I say unto thee, to-day shalt thou be with me in the paradise. And it was about the sixth hour, and there was a darkness over all the earth until the ninth hour. And the sun was darkened, and the veil of the temple was rent in the midst. And when Jesus had cried with a loud voice, he said, Father, into thy hands I commend my spirit: and having said thus, he gave up the ghost. Now when the centurion saw what was done, he glorified God, saying, Certainly this was a righteous man. And all the people that came together to that sight, beholding the things which were done, smote their breasts, and returned. And all his acquaintance, and the women that followed him from Galilee, stood afar off beholding these things.

Litany.

——o——

Psalm, cxliii, 1—12.

HEAR my prayer, O Lord; give ear to my supplications: in thy faithfulness answer me, and in thy righteousness. And enter not into judgment with thy servant: for in thy sight shall no man living be justified. For the enemy hath persecuted my soul: he hath smitten my life down to the ground; he hath made me to dwell in darkness, as those that have been long dead. Therefore is my spirit overwhelmed within me: my heart within me is desolate. I remember the days of old; I meditate on all thy works; I muse on the work of thy hands; I stretch forth my hands unto thee; my soul thirsteth after thee, as a thirsty land. Hear me speedily, O Lord; my spirit faileth: hide not thy face from me, lest I be like unto them that go down into the pit. Cause me to hear thy loving kindness in the morning: for in thee do I trust: cause me to know the way wherein I should walk; for I lift up my soul unto thee. Deliver me, O Lord, from mine enemies: I flee unto thee to hide me. Teach me to do thy will, for thou art my God: thy spirit is good; lead me into the land of uprightness. Quicken me, O Lord, for thy name's sake: for thy righteousness' sake bring my soul out of trouble. And of thy mercy cut off mine enemies, and destroy all them that afflict my soul: for I am thy servant.

Zechariah, xiv, 5—11.

AND the Lord my God shall come, and all the saints with thee. And it shall come to pass in that day that the light shall not be clear, nor dark: but it shall be one day which shall be known to the Lord, not day nor night: but it shall come to pass that at evening time it shall be light. And it shall be in that day that living waters shall go out from Jerusalem; half of them toward the former sea, and half of them toward the hinder sea; in summer and in winter shall it be. And the Lord shall be King over all the earth: in that day shall there be one Lord, and his name one. And the land shall be turned as a plain from Geba to Rimmon, south of Jerusalem; and it shall be lifted up, and inhabited in her place, from Benjamin's gate unto the place of the first gate, unto the corner gate, and from the tower of Hananeel unto the King's winepress. And men shall dwell in it, and there shall be no more utter destruction; but Jerusalem shall be safely inhabited.

I Timothy, vi, 13—16.

I GIVE the charge in the sight of God, who quickeneth all things, and before Christ Jesus, who before Pontius Pilate witnessed a good confession; that thou keep this commandment without spot, unrebukable, until the appearing of our Lord Jesus Christ: which in his times he shall shew, who is the blessed and only Potentate, the King of Kings, and Lords of Lords; who only hath immortality, dwelling in the light which no man can approach unto; whom no man hath seen, nor can see: to whom be honour and power everlasting. Amen.

St. John, xix, 17—37.

AND they took Jesus, and led him away. And he bearing his cross went forth into a place called the place of a skull, which is called in the Hebrew Golgotha, where they crucified him, and two other with him, on either side one, and Jesus in the midst. And Pilate wrote a title, and put it on the cross. And the writing was, Jesus of Nazareth, the King of the Jews. This title then read many of the Jews; for the

GOOD FRIDAY MIDDAY.

place where Jesus was crucified was nigh to the city: and it was written in Hebrew, and Greek, and Latin. Then said the chief priests of the Jews to Pilate, Write not the King of the Jews; but that he said I am King of the Jews. Pilate answered, What I have written I have written. Then the soldiers, when they had crucified Jesus, took his garments, and made four parts, to every soldier a part; and also his coat: now the coat was without seam, woven from the top throughout. They said therefore among themselves, Let us not rend it, but cast lots for it, whose it shall be: that the scripture might be fulfilled, which saith, They parted my raiment among them, and for my vesture they did cast lots. These things therefore the soldiers did. Now there stood by the cross of Jesus his mother, and his mother's sister, Mary the wife of Cleophas, and Mary Magdalene. When Jesus therefore saw his mother, and the disciple standing by, whom he loved, he saith unto his mother, Woman, behold thy son! Then saith he to the disciple, Behold thy mother! And from that hour that disciple took her unto his own home. after this, Jesus knowing that all things were now Acomplished, that the scripture might be fulfilled, with, I thirst. Now there was set a vessel full of vinegar: and they filled a sponge with vinegar, and put it upon hyssop and put it to his mouth. When Jesus therefore had received the vinegar, he said, It is finished: and he bowed his head, and gave up the ghost. The Jews, therefore, because it was the preparation, that the bodies should not remain upon the cross on the sabbath day (for that sabbath day was an high day), besought Pilate that their legs might be broken, and that they might be taken away. Then came the soldiers, and brake the legs of the first, and of the other which was crucified with him. But when they came to Jesus, and saw that he was dead already, they brake not his legs. But one of the soldiers with a spear pierced his side, and forthwith came there out blood and water. And he that saw it bare record, and his record is true : and he knoweth that he saith true that ye might believe. For these things were done, that the scripture should be fulfilled—a bone of him shall not be broken. And again another scripture saith, They shall look on him whom they pierced.

Ceremony of the Holy Cross with Hymns and Prayers.

———o———

EVENING SERVICE.

OUR Father. " Evening and morning, and at noon will I pray, and cry aloud : and he shall hear my voice."

Deacon : Let us pray to the Lord in peace. Receive us, save us, and have mercy upon us. (O Lord).

Priest : Blessing and glory to the Father, to the Son, and to the Holy Ghost, now and ever world without end. Amen.

GOOD FRIDAY EVENING.

Psalm, lxxxvi.

BOW down thine ear; O Lord, hear me: for I am poor and needy. (See page 198.)

Deacon: Let us pray to the Lord in peace. Receive us, save us, and have mercy upon us (O Lord).

Priest: Blessing and glory to the Father, to the Son, and to the Holy Ghost, now and ever, world without end. Amen.

Psalm, cxl.

DELIVER me, O Lord, from the evil man: preserve me from the violent man. (See page 199.)

Hymn.

---o---

Anthem.

THEY gave me also gall for my meat; and in my thirst they gave me vinegar to drink. Let their table become a snare before them: and that which shall have been for their welfare, let it become a trap.— *Psalm, lxix, 21, 22.*

Jeremiah, xi, 18—xii, 8.

AND the Lord hath given knowledge of it, and I know it; then thou shewedst me their doings. (See page 164.)

Isaiah, lii, 13—liii, 12.

BEHOLD, my servant shall deal prudently; he shall be exalted and extolled, and be very high. (See page 147.)

GOOD FRIDAY EVENING.

Psalm, xxii, 1—31.

MY God, my God, why hast thou forsaken me? (*See page* 141.)

Psalm, cxli, 2.

LET my prayer be set forth before thee as incense; and the lifting up of my hands as the evening sacrifice.

Litany.

———o———

Prayer by the Priest.

Trisagion. (*Kneeling down.*)

HOLY God, Holy and Mighty, Holy and Immortal, who wast crucified for us, have mercy upon us (*repeated thrice*).

———o———

Prayer by Priest.
Exhortation by Deacon.

———o———

Priest: Blessing and glory be to the Father, to the Son, and to the Holy Ghost, etc.

Psalm, cxxi.

I WILL lift up mine eyes unto the hills, from whence cometh my help.

———o———

Hymn of St. Isaac.
Prayer by Priest.

———o———

Psalm, xvi, 1.

FOR thou wilt not leave my soul in hell; neither wilt thou suffer thine Holy One to see corruption. Preserve me, O God: for in thee do I put my trust.

Wisdom of Solomon, ii, 1—22.

FOR the ungodly said, reasoning with themselves, but not aright, Our life is short and tedious, and in the death of a man there is no remedy: neither was there any man known to have returned from the grave. For we are born at all adventure: and we shall be hereafter as though we had never been: for the breath in our nostrils is as smoke, and a litttle spark in the moving of our heart: which being extinguished, our body shall be turned into ashes, and our spirit shall vanish as the soft air. And our name shall be forgotten in time, and no man shall have our works in remembrance, and our life shall pass away as the trace of a cloud, and shall be dispersed as a mist—that is, driven away with the beams of the sun, and overcome with the heat thereof. For our time is a very shadow that passeth away; and after our end there is no returning: for it is fast sealed, so that no man cometh again. Come on, therefore; let us enjoy the good things that are present; and let us speedily use the creatures like as in youth. Let us fill ourselves with costly wine and ointments: and let no flower of the spring pass by us. Let us crown ourselves with rosebuds, before they be withered. Let none of us go without his part of our voluptuousness : let us leave tokens of our joyfulness in every place : for this is our portion, and our lot is this. Let us oppress the poor righteous man, let us not spare the widow, nor reverence the ancient gray hairs of the aged. Let our strength be the law of justice : for that which is feeble is found to be nothing worth. Therefore let us lie in wait for the righteous; because he is not for our turn, and he is clean contrary to our doings: he upbraideth us with our offending the law, and objecteth to our infamy, the transgressions of our education. He professeth to have the knowledge of God : and he calleth himself the child of the Lord. He was made to reprove our thoughts. He is gracious unto us even to behold : for his life is not like other men's; his ways are of another fashion. We are esteemed of him as counterfeits : he abstaineth from our ways as from filthiness : he pronounceth the end of the just to be blessed, and maketh his boast that God is his father. Let us see if his words be true : and let us prove what shall happen in the end of him. For if the just man be the son of God, he will help him, and deliver him from the hand of his enemies. Let us examine him with despitefulness and torture, that we may know his meekness, and prove his patience. Let us condemn him with a shameful death : for by his own saying he shall be respected. Such things they did imagine, and were deceived: for their own wickedness hath blinded them. And for the mysteries of God, they knew them not: neither hoped they for the wages of righteousness, nor discerned a reward for blameless souls.

Zechariah, xii, 8—14.

IN that day shall the Lord defend the inhabitants of Jerusalem; and he that is feeble among them at that day shall be as David; and a house of David shall be as God, as the angel of the Lord before them. And it shall come to pass in that day that I will seek to destroy all the nations that come against Jerusalem. And I will pour upon the house of David and upon the inhabitants of Jerusalem the spirit of grace and of supplications: and they shall look upon me whom they have pierced, and they shall mourn for him, as one mourneth for his only son, and shall be in bitterness for him, as one that is in bitterness for his first-born. In that day shall there be a great mourning in Jerusalem, as the mourning of Hadadrimmon in the valley of Megiddon. And the land shall mourn, every family apart; the family of the house of David apart, and their wives apart; the family of the house of Nathan apart, and their wives apart; the family of the house of Levi apart, and their wives apart; the family of Shimei apart, and their wives apart; all the families that remain, every family apart, and their wives apart.

I Peter iii, 17—20.

FOR it is better, if the will of God be so, that ye suffer for well-doing, than for evil-doing. For Christ also hath once suffered for sins, the just for the unjust, that he might bring us to God, being put to death in the flesh, but quickened by the spirit: by which also he went and preached unto the spirits in prison; which sometimes were disobedient, when once the long suffering of God waiteth in the days of Noah, while the ark was a preparing, wherein few, that is, eight, souls were saved by water.

Alleluia, Alleluia.

WEEPING may endure for a night, but joy cometh in the morning.—*Psalm xxx, 5.*

St. Matthew, xxvii, 57—61.

WHEN the even was come, there came a rich man of Arimathea, named Joseph, who also himself was Jesus' disciple. He went to Pilate, and begged the body of Jesus. Then Pilate commanded the body to be delivered. And when Joseph had taken the body, he wrapped it in a clean linen cloth. And laid it in his own new tomb, which he had hewn out in the rock: and he rolled a great stone to the door of the sepulchre, and departed. And there was Mary Magdalene, and the other Mary, sitting over against the sepulchre.

—o—

Trisagion.

Holy God, Holy and Mighty, Holy and Immortal, Who wast Buried for us, have mercy upon us (repeated thrice.)

———o———

Celebration and Ceremony of the Burial of our Blessed Lord with Hymns and Prayers.

———o———

END.

———o———

Prayers composed by St. Nerses the Graceful in the year 1170, for every Believer in Christ.

I CONFESS with faith, and adore thee, O Father, Son, and Holy Ghost, increate and immortal Essence, Creator of Angels, of men, and of all that exists. Have mercy on thy creatures, and on me a grievous sinner.

2.—I confess with faith, and adore thee, O light indivisible, simultaneous, Holy Trinity, and one Godhead: creator of light and dispeller of darkness, dispel from my soul the darkness of sin and ignorance, and at this hour enlighten my mind, that I may pray to thee my petitions. Have mercy on thy creatures, and on me a grievous sinner.

3.—Heavenly Father, and true God, who didst send thy beloved Son to seek the lost sheep, I have sinned against heaven and before thee receive me like the prodigal son, and clothe me with that garment of which I was deprived by sin. Have mercy on thy creatures, and on me a grievous sinner.

4.—Son of God, and true God, who didst come down from the bosom of the Father, and wast incarnate of the Holy Virgin Mary for our redemption; wast crucified, and buried, and raised from the dead, and ascendedst to the Father, I have sinned against heaven, and before thee. Remember me like the penitent thief, when thou comest in thy kingdom. Have that are strangers to me, on my acquaintance, and on them that I know not, on the living and on the dead, and even forgive my enemies, and those that hate me, the trespasses they have committed against me, and turn them from that malice which they bear me, that they may be worthy of the mercy. Have mercy on thy creatures, and on me a grievous sinner.

24.—O Glorious Lord, receive the prayers of thy servant, and fulfil my petitions for my good, through the intercession of the Holy Mother of God, and John the Baptist, and the first Martyr Saint Stephen, and Saint Gregory our Illuminator, and the Holy Apostles, Prophets, Doctors, Martyrs, Patriarchs, Hermits, Virgins, and all thy Saints in Heaven and in Earth. Now unto Thee, O indivisible Holy Trinity, be glory and worship for ever and ever, Amen.

---o---

The Seven Penitential Psalms.

Prayers to be recited on Fasting days, and at other Penitential Times.

Psalm vi.

1. O Lord rebuke me not in thy indignation, nor chastise me in thy wrath.

2. Have mercy on me, O Lord, for I am weak: heal me, O Lord, for my bones are troubled.

3. And my soul is troubled exceedingly: but thou, O Lord, how long?

4. Turn to me, O Lord, and deliver my soul: oh, save me for thy mercy's sake.

5. For there is no one in death that is mindful of thee: and who shall confess to thee in hell?

6. I have laboured in my groanings; every night I will wash my bed: I will water my couch with my tears.

7. My eye is troubled through indignation: I have grown old amongst all my enemies.

8. Depart from me, all ye workers of iniquity; for the Lord hath heard the voice of my weeping.

9. The Lord hath heard my supplication: the Lord hath received my prayer.

10. Let my enemies be ashamed, and be very much troubled: let them be turned back, and be ashamed very speedily.

Glory be to the Father, etc.

Psalm xxxi.

1. Blessed are they whose iniquities are forgiven, and whose sins are covered.

2. Blessed is the man to whom the Lord hath not imputed sin, and in whose spirit there is no guile.

3. Because I was silent, my bones grew old; whilst I cried out all the day long.

4. For day and night thy hand was heavy upon me: I am turned in my anguish, whilst the thorn is fastened.

5. I have acknowledged my sin to thee: and my injustice I have not concealed.

6. I said I will confess against myself my injustice to the Lord; and thou hast forgiven the wickedness of my sin.

7. For this shall every one that is holy pray to thee in a seasonable time.

8. And yet in a flood of many waters they shall not come nigh unto him.

9. Thou art my refuge from the trouble which hath encompassed me; my joy, deliver me from them that surround me.

10. I will give thee understanding, and I will instruct thee in the way in which thou shalt go; I will fix my eyes upon thee.

11. Do not become like the horse and the mule, who have no understanding.

12. With bit and bridle bind fast their jaws, who come not near unto thee.

13. Many are the scourges of the sinner, but mercy shall encompass him that hopeth in the Lord.

14. Be glad in the Lord, and rejoice, ye just; and glory, all ye right of heart.

Glory be to the Father, etc.

Psalm xxxvii.

1. Rebuke me not, O Lord, in thy indignation, nor chastise me in thy wrath.

2. For thy arrows are fastened in me, and thy hand hath been strong upon me.

3. There is no health in my flesh, because of thy wrath; there is no peace for my bones, because of my sins.

4. For my iniquities are gone over my head; and, as a heavy burden, are become heavy upon me.

5. My sores are putrefied and corrupted, because of my foolishness.

6. I am become miserable, and am bowed down even to the end; I walked sorrowful all the day long.

7. For my loins are filled with illusions, and there is no health in my flesh.

8. I am afflicted and humbled exceedingly; I roared with the groaning of my heart.

9. Lord, all my desire is before thee, and my groaning is not hidden from thee.

10. My heart is troubled, my strength hath left me, and the light of my eyes itself is not with me.

11. My friends and my neighbours have drawn near and stood against me.

12. And they that were near me stood afar off; and they that sought my soul used violence.

13. And they that sought evils to me, spoke vain things, and studied deceits all the day long.

14. But I, as a deaf man, heard not; as a dumb man not opening his mouth.

15. And I became as a man that heareth not, and that hath no reproofs in his mouth.

16. For in thee, O Lord, have I hoped; thou wilt hear me, O Lord my God.

17. For I said: Lest at any time my enemies rejoice over me; and whilst my feet are moved, they speak great things against me.

18. For I am ready for scourges, and my sorrow is continually before me.

19. For I will declare my iniquity; and I will think for my sin.

20. But my enemies live and are stronger than I; and they that hate me wrongfully are multiplied.

21. They that render evil for good have detracted me, because I followed goodness.

22. Forsake me not, O Lord my God; do not thou depart from me.

23. Attend unto my help, O Lord, the God of my salvation. Glory, etc.

Psalm l.

1. Have mercy on me, O God, according to thy great mercy.

2. And according to the multitude of thy tender mercies, blot out my iniquity.

3. Wash me yet more from my iniquity and cleanse me from my sin.

4. For I know my iniquity, and my sin is always before me.

5. To thee only have I sinned, and have done evil before thee; that thou mayest be justified in thy words, and mayest overcome when thou art judged.

6. For behold I was conceived in iniquities; and in sin did my mother conceive me.

7. For behold thou hast loved truth; the uncertain and hidden things of thy wisdom thou hast made manifest to me.

8. Thou shalt sprinkle me with hyssop, and I shall be cleansed; thou shalt wash me, and I shall be made whiter than snow.

9. To my hearing thou shalt give joy and gladness; and the bones that have been humbled shall rejoice.

10. Turn away thy face from my sins, and blot out my iniquities.

11. Create a clean heart in me, O God; and renew a right spirit within my bowels.

12. Cast me not away from thy face; and take not thy holy spirit from me.

13. Restore unto me the joy of thy salvation, and strengthen me with a perfect spirit.

14. I will teach the unjust thy ways; and the wicked shall be converted to thee.

15. Deliver me from blood, O God, thou God of my salvation; and my tongue shall extol thy justice.

16. O Lord, thou wilt open my lips; and my mouth shall declare thy praise.

17. For if thou hadst desired sacrifice, I would indeed have given it ; with burnt offerings thou wilt not be delighted.

18. A sacrifice to God is an afflicted spirit: a contrite and humbled heart, O God, thou wilt not despise.

19. Deal favourably, O Lord, in thy goodness with Sion ; that the walls of Jerusalem may be built up.

20. Then shalt thou accept the sacrifice of justice, oblations and whole burnt-offerings ; then shall they lay calves upon thy altar.

Glory, etc.

Psalm, ci.

1. Hear, O Lord, my prayer, and let my cry come to thee.

2. Turn not away thy face from me ; in the day when I am in trouble, incline thine ear to me.

3. In what day soever I shall call upon thee, hear me speedily.

4. For my days are vanished like smoke ; and my bones are grown dry, like fuel for the fire.

5. I am smitten as grass, and my heart is withered ; because I forgot to eat my bread.

6. Through the voice of my groaning, my bone hath cleaved to my flesh.

7. I am become like to a pelican of the wilderness ; I am like a night-raven in the house.

8. I have watched, and am become as a sparrow all alone on the house-top.

9. All the day long my enemies reproached me; and they that praised me did swear against me.

10. For I did eat ashes like bread, and mingled my drink with weeping.

11. Because of thy anger and indignation? for having lifted me up thou hast thrown me down.

12. My days have declined like a shadow, and I am withered like grass.

13. But thou, O Lord, endurest for ever; and thy memorial to all generations.

14. Thou shalt arise and have mercy on Sion: for it is time to have mercy on it, for the time is come.

15. For the stones thereof have pleased thy servants; and they shall have pity on the earth thereof.

16. And the Gentiles shall fear thy name, O Lord; and all the kings of the earth thy glory.

17. For the Lord hath built up Sion; and he shall be seen in his glory.

18. He hath had regard to the prayer of the humble; and he hath not despised their petition.

19. Let these things be written unto another generation; and the people that shall be created shall praise the Lord.

20. Because he hath looked forth from his high sanctuary; from heaven the Lord hath looked upon the earth.

21. That he might hear the groans of them that are in fetters; that he might release the children of the slain.

22. That they may declare the name of the Lord in Sion: and his praise in Jerusalem.

23. When the people assembled together, and kings to serve the Lord.

24. He answered him in the way of his strength: Declare unto me the fewness of my days.

25. Call me not away in the midst of my days; thy years are unto generation and generation.

26. In the beginning, O Lord, thou foundest the earth; and the heavens are the work of thy hands.

27. They shall perish, but thou remainest, and all of them shall grow old like a garment:

28. And as a vesture thou shalt change them, and they shall be changed. But thou art always the selfsame, and thy years shall not fail:

29. The children of thy servants shall continue; and their seed shall be directed for ever.

Glory, etc.

Psalm cxxix.

1. Out of the depths I have cried to thee, O Lord; Lord, hear my voice.

2. Let thy ears be attentive to the voice of my supplication.

3. If thou wilt observe iniquities, O Lord: Lord, who shall endure it?

4. For with thee there is merciful forgiveness: and by reason of thy law, I have waited for thee, O Lord.

5. My soul hath relied on his word: my soul hath hoped in the Lord.

6. From the morning watch, even until night, let Israel hope in the Lord.

7. Because with the Lord there is mercy, and with him plentiful redemption.

8. And he shall redeem Israel from all his iniquities.

Glory, etc.

Psalm, cxlii.

1. Hear, O Lord, my prayers: give ear to my supplication in thy truth; hear me in thy justice.

2. And enter not into judgment with thy servant; for in thy sight no man living shall be justified.

3. For the enemy hath persecuted my soul; he hath brought down my life to the earth.

4. He hath made me to dwell in darkness, as those that hath been dead of old; and my spirit is in anguish within me; my heart within me is troubled.

5. I remember the days of old: I meditated on all thy works; I meditated upon the works of thy hands.

6. I stretched forth my hands to thee; my soul is as earth without water unto thee.

7. Hear me speedily, O Lord; my spirit hath fainted away.

8. Turn not away thy face from me, lest I be like unto them that go down into the pit.

9. Cause me to hear thy mercy in the morning ; for in thee have I hoped.

10. Make thy way known to me wherein I should walk ; for I have lifted up my soul to thee.

11. Deliver me from my enemies, O Lord, to thee have I fled.

12. Teach me to do thy will, for thou art my God.

13. Thy good spirit shall lead me into the right land ; for thy name's sake, O Lord, thou wilt quicken me in thy justice.

14. Thou wilt bring my soul out of trouble ; and in thy mercy thou wilt destroy my enemies.

15. And thou wilt cut off all them that afflict my soul ; for I am thy servant.

Glory be to the Father, etc.

Ant. Remember not, O Lord, our offences, nor those of our parents ; neither take thou vengeance on our sins.

---o---

Psalm, lxxxvi.

BOW down thine ear, O Lord, hear me: for I am poor and needy. Preserve my soul; for I am holy: O thou my God, save thy servant that trusteth in thee. Be merciful unto me, O Lord: for I cry unto thee daily. Rejoice the soul of thy servant: for unto thee, O Lord, do I lift up my soul. For thou, Lord, art good, and ready to forgive; and plenteous in mercy unto all them that call upon thee. Give ear, O Lord, unto my prayer; and attend to the voice of my supplications. In the day of my trouble I will call upon thee: for thou wilt answer me. Among the gods there is none like unto thee, O Lord; neither are there any works like unto thy works. All nations whom thou hast made shall come and worship before thee, O Lord; and shall glorify thy name. For thou art great, and doest wondrous things: thou art God alone. Teach me thy way, O Lord; I will walk in thy truth: unite my heart to fear thy name. I will praise thee O Lord my God, with all my heart: and I will glorify thy name for evermore. For great is thy mercy toward me: and thou hast delivered my soul from the lowest hell. O God, the proud are risen against me, and the assemblies of violent men have sought after my soul; and have not set thee before them. But thou, O Lord, art a God full of compassion, and gracious, long suffering, and plenteous in mercy and truth. O turn unto me, and have mercy upon me:

give thy strength unto thy servant, and save the son of thine handmaid. Shew me a token for good; that they which hate me may see it, and be ashamed: because thou, Lord, hast holpen me, and comforted me.

Glory to the Father, etc.

A short prayer by the Priest.
Exhortation by the Deacon.

Priest: Blessing and glory be to the Father, to the Son and to the Holy Ghost.

Psalm, cxl.

DELIVER me, O Lord, from the evil man: preserve me from the violent man; which imagine mischiefs in their heart; continually are they gathered together for war. They have sharpened their tongue like a serpent; adder's poison is under their lips. Selah. Keep me, O Lord, from the hands of the wicked; preserve me from the violent man; who have purposed to overthrow my goings. The proud have hid a snare for me, and cords; they have spread a net by the wayside; they have set gins for me. Selah. I said unto the Lord, thou art my God: hear the voice of my supplications, O Lord. O God the Lord, the strength of my salvation, thou hast covered my head in the day of battle. Grant not, O Lord, the desires of the wicked: further not his wicked device; lest they exalt themselves. Selah. As for the head of those that compass me about, let the mischief of their own lips cover them. Let burning coals fall upon them: let them be cast into the fire; into deep pits, that they rise not up again. Let not an evil speaker be established in the earth: evil shall hunt the violent man to overthrow him. I know that the Lord will maintain the cause of the afflicted, and the right of the poor. Surely the righteous shall give thanks unto thy name; the upright shall dwell in thy presence.

Psalm, cxli.

LORD, I cry unto thee: make haste unto me; give ear unto my voice, when I cry unto thee. Let my prayer be set forth before thee as incense; and the lifting up of my hands as the evening sacrifice. Set a watch, O Lord, before my mouth; keep the door of my lips. Incline not my heart to any evil thing, to practise wicked works with men that work iniquity: and let me not eat of their dainties. Let the righteous smite me; it shall be a kindness: and let him reprove me; it shall be an excellent oil, which shall not break my head: for yet my prayer also shall be in their calamities. When their judges are overthrown in stony places, they shall hear my words; for they are sweet. Our bones are scattered at the grave's mouth, as when one cutteth and cleaveth wood upon the earth. But mine eyes are unto thee, O God the Lord: in thee is my trust; leave not my soul destitute. Keep me from the snares which they have laid for me, and the gins of the workers of iniquity. Let the wicked fall into their own nets, whilst that I withal escape.

Psalm, cxlii.

I CRIED unto the Lord with my voice, with my voice unto the Lord did I make my supplication. I poured out my complaint before him: I shewed before him my trouble. When my spirit was overwhelmed within me, then thou knewest my path. In the way wherein I walked have they privily laid a snare for me. I looked on my right hand, and beheld, but there was no man that would know me: refuge failed me; no man cared for my soul. I cried unto thee, O Lord: I said, thou art my refuge and my portion in the land of the living. Attend unto my cry; for I am brought very low: deliver me from my persecutors; for they are stronger than I. Bring my soul out of prison, that I may praise thy name; the righteous shall compass me about; for thou shalt deal bountifully with me.

Glory be to the Father, etc.

———o———

Prayer by the Priest.
Exhortation by Deacon.
A short prayer by the Priest.

———o———

(Here follows the Anthem, etc. See page 40.*)*

www.ingramcontent.com/pod-product-compliance
Lightning Source LLC
Chambersburg PA
CBHW020824230426
43666CB00007B/1099